POETRY IN

MICHIGAN

IN POETRY

Edited by William Olsen & Jack Ridl

New Issues Poetry & Prose
The College of Arts and Sciences
Western Michigan University
Kalamazoo, Michigan 49008

First Edition, 2013.

ISBN: 978-1-936970-16-2 (hardcover)

Library of Congress Cataloging-in-Publication Data:
New Issues Poetry & Prose
Poetry in Michigan / Michigan in Poetry/New Issues Poetry & Prose
Library of Congress Control Number: 2013931587

Editors:	William Olsen and Jack Ridl
Managing Editor:	Kimberly Kolbe
Copy Editor:	Allison Lee
Design:	Paul Sizer
Production:	Sizer Design + Illustration
	www.paulsizer.com
Printing:	McNaughton & Gunn, Inc.

This activity is supported in part by an award from the Michigan Council for Arts and Cultural Affairs
and the National Endowment for the Arts, and Bell's Brewery.

TABLE OF CONTENTS

Introduction by Jim Daniels

An Introduction to
"Poetry in Michigan/Michigan in Poetry"

William Olsen and Jack Ridl have put together a wonderful selection here that reflects the voices and landscapes of one of the most distinct of the fifty states. While all states are distinct in some ways, it's hard to top Michigan. It certainly is "home" to a lot of fine poets.

The novelist and screenwriter Richard Price once said that where you're from is "…the zip code for your heart." When it comes to Michigan, this seems true for all of these poets. Some are not Michigan natives, and others have moved out of state, but Michigan has found a way inside their hearts. Michigan is like that. It's not just any one thing, but the complexity of the place—of its many places—that resonates. From the often-struggling city of Detroit with its difficult history of race relations, and its economic ups and downs, to the rugged, natural terrain and tough winters of the Upper Peninsula (the U.P.), Michigan offers many intricate human and physical challenges for these poets to explore.

I've lived in Pennsylvania since 1981, and while I love the city of Pittsburgh, I have no sense of being a "Pennsylvanian." In fact, I don't know if I've heard of anyone refer to themselves with this term, while, despite the inherent goofiness of the term, many people refer to themselves as Michiganders. I do. It's hard to explain. David Dodd Lee writes about "suffering being somehow/ different in, say, Texas, than it is here in Michigan, where pain/comes draped in silver and silence."

While Michigan poets certainly take pride in their state, what strikes me about so many of these poems is their humility—humility in the face of extreme weather, hard winters; humility in the face of economic hardship; humility in the face of the challenges of daily life—challenges stemming from unpredictability of both the human and natural worlds.

Stylistically, these poets are all over the poetic map, with incantations, reflections, stories—from the exuberance of Linda Nemec Foster to the careful noticing and recording of Dan Gerber. But I was struck by how all these poems are *about* something, some *place*. The groundedness of these poems is reassuring. The Michigan in them is a place with no room for idle word-play—snow has to be shoveled, leaves have to be raked, and somebody has to bring home a paycheck.

These poets discover and celebrate the state beyond the tourist slogans: "Pure Michigan," "Say Yes to Michigan," "A Water-Winter Wonderland," "Great Lakes, Great Times," "The Great Lakes

State." James Armstrong addresses this head-on in his poem, "Say Yes to Michigan," in which the speaker admits to sometimes "growing weary of/ too-much scenery, pines and lakes that/ overwhelm, a surfeit of jet-skis, too/many winking, perfect cherries."

It is not so much the search for beauty that drives these poets, but the surprise of finding it in unlikely places. francine j. harris writes:

> She said I live in Detroit. And there are no flowers in Detroit.
> So why would anyone in Detroit write about flowers in Detroit.
>
> I don't tell her we live under the trees. Root up curbs and dam fire hydrants
> to water black pansies licked to the sides of popped black balloons in Detroit.

These poets are not cheerleaders or sloganeers—they're digging things up, cutting things open. They're watching people die, they're falling in love, just like poets everywhere, but they're doing it here, where black ice can send them suddenly skidding out of control. The poems explore how we connect, attach and detach from place. Poets have no slogans. Or, if they do, they constantly contradict them.

It may not be surprising to see how frequently bodies of water—the Great Lakes, of course, and the many rivers and inland lakes—show up in these poems. Anyone who has spent time in Michigan knows Christine Rhein's "wet smell/of the world." It is said that you are never more than six miles from a body of water in Michigan; the influence of water is large and compelling in this anthology. These poems often find the unexpected discoveries in the familiar, as in this odd, wrenching moment from "Change," by Cullen Bailey Burns: "Once we watched a deer swim out into Lake Michigan./Twilight and the deer kept swimming/toward the sinking sun."

We are all drawn to the water—it gives life, takes it away. It is full of magic and mystery—Peter Markus writes, "In the darkness of the river we'd hear these stones go plunk and plunk." Linda Gregerson seems to speak to both the spiritual aspect of water and our inability to tame it when she writes: "It's heartening/to think a river makes some difference."

The natural world also figures prominently in these poems in the seasonal changes. Everyone everywhere talks about the weather, and comparing the weather to emotional states in poetry is nothing new, but in Michigan the weather is much more than idle conversation or an easy trope. We have a stake in our weather, our distinct, dramatic seasons, and that translates into an intense attention to and reverence for the naming of things—birds, trees, flowers, animals, fish. In Jim Harrison's "Walking" alone, we get: poplar, scrub oak, a gully, a knoll, a ridge, a trough, a spring, a pine stump, a basswood swale, deer, ferns, a blue racer, mosquitoes, birches, grasshoppers, birds, grass, a Cooper's hawk, a crow, lake shore, blackberry, sumac, lily pads, sweet moss, gravel, whippoorwills, reeds, frogs, alders, hay bales, hardwoods, cedars, and a small spring. These poets connect to the landscapes by identifying the things in them, savoring the names as a kind of prayer we whisper in reverence or desperation.

Of course, these poets aren't just describing scenery—they are also making a living. M.L. Liebler writes, "Here, it's always/Work—Not talk. We know that/Talk is cheap, but work is/Forever." Some of that work involves serving the needs of tourists, as in Greg Rappleye's poem, "Thousand Dollar Days," a portrait of his father at his root beer stand in northern Michigan that serves "teenaged kids,/ on vacation with their parents/from the suburbs of Detroit.":

> in a tourist town,
> *traffic* is what matters.
> So my father lays his pen down
> to watch the passing cars, subtracting out
> the junky Fords and pickups of the locals.

And many of those who come up north from the Motor City work in the auto industry. The speaker in Philip Levine's "A Dozen Dawn Songs, Plus One," describes his memories of that hard work: "It's still Monday/2,000 miles and fifty years/later and at my back I always/hear Chevy Gear & Axle/grinding the night shift workers/into antiquity."

Junky Fords, Chevy Gear and Axle. The list of proper names that appear in these poems is like a litany, a song, a prayer: Kilmer's Lake, Spider Lake, Savage's Lake, Well's Lake, Manistee, Marquette, Detroit, Burt Lake, Lake Michigan, Detroit, Rochester, Warren, Whitefish Point, Copper Harbor, Did I say Detroit?, the DNR, Kalamazoo, Flat Rock, Wyandotte, Cathead Point, Port Oneida, North Bar Lake, Eastern Market, Lake Superior, Mackinac Bridge, Detroit River, Au Sable, Glen Lake, North Fishtail Bay, Lansing, Palmer, Cadillac, Kalkaska, Three Rivers, Fords, Thunderbird, Galaxie, Mazda, (Mazda?!), Chevy, Lincoln Continental, General Motors, Sleeping Bear Dunes, Misery Bay, Woodward, Grand River, I-75, the John Lodge, 7 Mile Road, Livernois, Baker's Keyboard Lounge, South Haven, Temptations, Smokey Robinson, Amen.

Amen. This collection should have a readership well beyond Michigan, for our state has a mystique that makes it attractive to everyone. Few people drive through Michigan to get somewhere else. It is a destination. It is a border. It is a shoreline. It is a mitten—a soft mitten, with hard edges. A mitten attached by the beautiful strand of the Mackinac Bridge to whatever shape you want to dream up for the U.P.

Ander Monson, in "Vacationland," speaks for many of the poets when he describes his relationship to Michigan:

> Everyone from here is still from here
> regardless of where they are or where they end.
> ....
> This vacationland, this Michigan,
> my Michigan, is no destination, no getaway
> for us, those who are always *from*.

I could celebrate every single poem in here—a rare statement to make about any anthology. Leave it to the poets to find the heart of a place. This book will make you fall in love with Michigan all over again, or for the first time. Those who are "from" welcome you to these pages.

—Jim Daniels

MYSTERY STAIRWAY
Michelle Calkins

At Burt Lake

Tom Andrews

To disappear into the right words
and to be their meanings. . .

October dusk.
Pink scraps of clouds, a plum-colored sky.
The sycamore tree spills a few leaves.
The cold focuses like a lens. . .

Now night falls, its hair
caught in the lake's eye.

Such clarity of things. Already
I've said too much. . .

       Lord,
language must happen to you
the way this black pane of water,
chipped and blistered with stars,
happens to me.

SAY YES TO MICHIGAN

James Armstrong

Say it. Please. I
absolve you if you are lying.
You don't feel enthusiastic?
You don't want to be false?
Even I sometimes feel that way: less than
sanguine, wanting less, growing weary of
too-much scenery, pines and lakes that
overwhelm, a surfeit of jet-skis, too
many winking, perfect cherries.
I sometimes want to be alone
crossing the urban street and
having a thought which is not recreational
in the least: brooding, or feeling a
gust of grief; that's ok. But arrowed
(as we must be) toward the next
near moment, kept by default from
no, isn't it easier to say *yes*? Embrace the
obvious, which can't be your fault,
which can't be voided or fought?

CHANGE

Cullen Bailey Burns

Once we watched a deer swim out into Lake Michigan.
Twilight and the deer kept swimming
toward the sinking sun.

Fall is in the air this morning, in the breath
that rises from the children waiting for the school bus
and its noisy rows of those

who were us, we know, looking down
into our coffee cups, and who will one day
be us again—early morning,

work clothes on, coffee steaming
from the cup. Called the DNR about the deer.
It was August. The sand grew cold

beneath our feet as the sun went down
and we stood watching. The DNR said it just happens
sometimes, the swimming out and then

the fear. Can't do a thing.
And here's the bus. My daughter is too old
to look back as she climbs up

in the golden light that makes us beautiful.
There's no one to call for help. The deer
swam straight at that sun.

Such transmutation: water, sky, gold.

THIS PERFECT PLACE
David Grath

FREIGHTERS RETURN TO THE HARBOR

Jackie Bartley

A sure sign of spring. Their massive hulls
              dwarf men on deck and on the docks
      working chutes into place to deliver

limestone, coal, and sand. Or guiding the scrap
              yard's magnetized arm
      to heave great fistsfuls of metal on board.

Each freighter's deep, watery bass sounds
              as it navigates the narrows,
      passes through the channel, glides atop

the lake's inconstant swells. Heading west,
              their pitch and yaw suggest
      the living bulk of whales setting out on long

migrations, baleful cries echoing hundreds of miles,
              pod to pod until the ocean becomes
      one animal-mind.

A Lilliputian crew perches on the stern for a last
              glimpse of land until morning.
      Commerce, cargo, and shifting waves

mark the hours. Nights, we listen to their lament
              fading into dreams on the border
      of memory, cavernous vessel that carries us.

That sometimes swallows us whole.

THE BURN

Elinor Benedict

Each July and August blueberry pickers prowl
this barren tract that burned five years ago. Folks
say flames ate acres of jack pine, fed blackened sand
whatever wild berries need to grow, thick as anyone

could plant. Across the clustered fields
whole families dot the hazy green. They bend
their backs willingly to the punishing sun, laugh
and call out to each other, hot and happy

in the face-slapping blaze, getting something rich
for nothing. Now here I come, two weeks late,
a lone gleaner with hands in pockets, wandering
the plains, thinking how quickly autumn and winter

return. A chill breeze rises, fresh but foreign,
like air restless over old battlefields long turned
to grass. I look for whatever's left, expecting
famine after all those hands, weeks of dust,

last night's deluge. But wait: here, there, spots
of blue on green pop up all over, plenty for me
to pick and eat until dark. Then in a flickering
of grace I see Thanksgiving's fabled horn

tumbling with apples, oranges, and grapes,
possessed by blue magic enough to feed
every last picker on earth until snow
sifts down and covers us all.

LANDSCAPE IN BLUE AND GREY
Stephen Magsig

DOWN IN DETROIT

Terry Blackhawk

"Help me! I live in Detroit."
> Sign taped to a tip cup on the popcorn counter
> of the Maple Art Theater in Bloomfield Hills, Michigan, 2003

Remember when the flight attendant had us prepare
for landing in "Honolu…oops, Detroit"
and the whole plane laughed?
And did I tell you the one about the ex-
Michigander who turned her back on me
& pointedly bestowed her life story (Border Collies
and Harry Potter included) on another woman
waiting for the Napa Shuttle after I winced
& replied yes, yes, **in** Detroit, I live
IN Detroit. Or the librarian from Oakland Hills:
his "You live down in Detroit?" still echoes
down, down, down.
                    Tough enough to love
this town without the shocked looks, dropped
jaws of fellow citizens who assume whiteness
unites as they eye you, reassessing instantly. Still,
"The D" — dear "D" — must have some magic in it.
How else explain the doubled take, the suddenly shed
disguise? In less than an eye-blink, I've had men
switch from flirt to default mode, their mental
U-turns screeching with chagrin.   Such power
in a word: to make a person give himself away.

Dee-troit, *day–twah*, strait in French, place where waters
move swiftly.

Setting Up the Fountain in Rochester Municipal Park: Late May

Gladys Cardiff

7 a.m. on a weekday, and I'm not happy to find
the park bristling with park personnel emptying the
    trash bins, policing the walks. I like the park quieter.
Yet, the trees hold their branches out invitingly,
    and a mallard on a mission, sharp as morning air, struts over
        my disappointment, her first brood
a squad of jumbo bumblebees trailing behind her, so I fall
    in line and follow her six fuzzballs to the bank
    of the pond, and watch the bluegill dart, backing
off their nests to wait beneath the algae mat. I'm here for the small

sounds and guiltless schemes, like the ant, gladiatorial, that hefts
his trophy, the carapace of a two-striped grasshopper, against the sky.
    I'm wary of the crew driving up, unloading a Jon boat on the grass.
But they are beautiful, going about their work, assembling some machinery,
    clearly, a routine for them, one they do without any fuss,
        two men companionable over the valves and jets,
a third bankside, doing some magic. *Voila.* A box pops up,
    and the boat trails an umbilical cord as it drifts to the middle.
    The sun is high and hot. The squirrels
lope off to their hideaways for an afternoon nap.

And now, a man in a wheelchair, wearing a camouflage jacket
parks next to me, staying, like me, to watch the men do their work.
    And there it is. What these preparations mean. I feel his bulk and breathe
his funk, an old man smell you, our dearest, will never have. The men sink
    four anchor weights, one for each cardinal direction and out drops grief
and bitterness, the sleeper awakened, that never lets
go. A column gushes up, shrugs, then pads the whitening air, spumes crystal
    shards into the blue. Beautiful, the fountain tableau of four men
    shaking hands. Awakened, the weighty thing, curled in a question
mark, settling in the mud below, tooled to serve our projects when we call.

SUBWAY PASSENGER, MOSCOW, RUSSIA 2012
Nathan Caplan

Mother as Opalescent Bottle

Susanna Childress

Upon falling in love with her, this time in Michigan,
where autumn comes sooner than expected

You sit in the breakfast nook, soundless as the panicle
        of the final red phlox outside the window; you have noticed
small veins beginning to rise over the knuckles and back

of your hand. You are not yet thirty, are not thinking *age*. Once,
        long ago, in church, you sat this way, pressing the veins
of your mother's hand, that web of emerald channels, resilient under

your thumb, pressing down, around, over, like the nose
        of a deer into wild blackberry bush, thinking *this is*, until
your mother's other hand would reach over to still you

and she would nod, slow as the opening tilt of a paper fan,
        toward the preacher. Here, where you are, a glass of water held
as though it were a nuthatch between your knees, the sun's

long, last slant across the back deck, the bowl of chrysanthemums
        dare September to snuff them out and your neighbor's boys
alternate shouting *Die-die-die* with *Ay'ay, Cap'n!* on a trampoline

that yawns them up and snatches them back while they clash
        branches torn from the sagging Sugar Maple. One
of them is crying, voices dissolve as salt in broth but then,

as quickly, begin again. Above them, a black squirrel runs
        the telephone wire with a brilliant ear of corn
in its mouth. All this is part of your mother's body—

that opalescent bottle, that absolute pulchritude, yes, each
        necessary furbelow. You could not find such Latinate words
even if you wanted to, will not, perhaps, until the first snow.

Missing

Patricia Clark

How can I go down to the river,
nudge the car into my usual spot, and walk?
How can I set the brake and clip the leash
onto the dog's collar?

While he's lost, how can I go on stepping
along the riverbank? The path curves, near
the lagoon, and I go with it. I count the mallards,
always in pairs, most domestic of the ducks.

He's lost somewhere in the river,
boat found, shoes and creel found, but he
himself lost between Rockford and the blue bridge
at Fulton Street. How can I go easy?

While he's lost it doesn't seem right
to walk without aim, to study swollen buds
on the willows and oaks, to long for the ground
softening, for the spears of green to come.

How can I go easy down to the river, water
where I dipped my hand after my father died,
river that I asked to soothe him,
and now the river that has taken this life?

Rivers are where my brothers stand in their tall
hipboots, lines swishing out like the lithe tongues
of frogs to nab a tasty bug, rivers where
my father stood, seeking quiet away from home.

One day a red helicopter clattered along overhead,
low and looking, and it wasn't a time to wave.
They went searching along the riverbank. It wasn't my
brother they looked for, but it might have been.

How can I go down to the river, tomorrow, today,
drive down and steer the car into a spot,
knowing that he's lost in water cold
as slate, soul seeking for a way to climb out?

THE DHARMA AT LAST

David Cope

long dead in his dream the boys leap
    one by one over the cliff into the wild splash
        & the singing current—the tow pulling them

    down into green dark & silt where the sunken
trees fell & were pinned as well, great black
    branches looming up in the murk, fish tearing

        the guts of whitened & bloated corpses as
    their eyes stared, marbled spheres like moons
glowing in the dark. by night, the water clears, the

shadow moon reflects off the pale carcasses—
        & he is awake, panting, the moon shining
    thru his midnight window. he hears the voices of

thousands singing & weeping as police line up
    & swat batons swat batons swat batons & march
        march march into the now-screaming singers,

    their ranks breaking—the one-eyed bard chanting
for calm—the ranks all fled, he left alone to sweat on
    a factory floor, in a madhouse swabbing urinals. now

        the dreams are all moonlit, no destination
    & yet this weary traveler sings in his passing
steps, careless in the theatre of stars where the dead

    walk with him daily, nightly, old companions
        urging him to rest as even days grow darker,
    the news ever more ominous. he must consider

the sleek craft of his final voyages, the turns in his
    last river, the song he will compose to take him
            beyond his last lay to sing in dreams where

    his companions fled, to learn to walk among
the living like a shadow in the daylight of
    their certainties, waiting for them to leap at last.

DARK SPACES

Meridith Ridl

Aerial View of Warren, Michigan

Jim Daniels

We played Monopoly in our dark, damp,
unfinished basements, lining up tiny green houses
like gods or general contractors.

Like those houses, ours were identical.
Our favorite songs repeated endless nonsense
syllables. We couldn't get enough sameness,
walking blind-folded into each other's bathrooms

because—because we knew! Rolling the dice—
badoom badoom badoom. Hard splash
onto the square board. We hoarded get-out-of-jail-
free cards. We fought over who'd be banker.

We cheated with careful abandon. We purchased
hotels reluctantly, the big red loneliness on all
that space, no open-windowed neighbors screaming.

We stood on stoops and called each other out to play.
We did not trust doorbells or any closed door.
Anyone with a piano or a dog of recognizable breed.

Four boys hunched at the board in dusty light,
a whiff of mold, the reckless chirping of a cricket.
Our fathers who art at the factory. No getting lost.
No shortcuts, no twisting paths, no maze of greenery.

Once we cut windows and doors in a refrigerator box.
We rolled it back and forth against the fence.
We bounced our loose limbs off each other.
A mobile home! We joyfully tore it up.

We loved rolling doubles. The dotted lines
of two sixes. We did not understand the concept
of Free Parking or Luxury Tax. Or even Monopoly!

$200 each time we rounded the block?
It'd just make us dizzy. We had a lot to learn,
but no way were we going to summer school.
We were living it up in Marvin's Gardens!

We constructed basement boxing rings
and smacked each other till we finally
got mad. Whatever adults existed upstairs
pretended they didn't hear.

I know I have stretched the truth about the streets
of Warren, Michigan. Like if I told you Larry Warren
glued all the Monopoly houses down

so we couldn't get them unstuck without ripping
up the board. You can only stretch the truth so far
till it snaps like the rubber band around Chance cards.

If you're passing over in a helicopter or small plane
out of perversity or emergency, you could look
down and see the tiny people emerging
from the tiny houses to wave or give you the finger

or both. We would expect an equally appropriate gesture,
all of us down here—the Iron, the Shoe, the Dog and Wheelbarrow.
Even that weird dude, the Top Hat, a rabbit in each hand,
alone on the corner where we ditched him.

Letter to Jim Harrison

Michael Delp

Dear Jim,

Sometimes the world is all teeth, no rest, empty buckets where there used to be enough liquid to keep me going another week or so. When I was in college I wrote a bad poem about a guy who could take out his own heart. At night he'd hang it in a tree in an onion sack so the coyotes could sit under it and dream their mouths into its flesh. In the poem he said that all day he could feel their breath in his chest, and he considered himself anointed, fueled, he actually recalled, as if he could run down anything. So, in this poem, that's what he did. Ran things down, came to think of himself as some kind of half-human woods god with a huge heart and plenty of scores to settle. That's where it ended, that half of a poem, with him sitting under a tree in a swamp, his heart pounding its way, literally out of his chest.

WINTER CATTAILS II
Lois Lovejoy

THE WEAKNESS

Toi Derricotte

That time my grandmother dragged me
through the perfume aisles at Saks, she held me up
by my arm, hissing, "Stand up,"
through clenched teeth, her eyes
bright as a dog's
cornered in the light.
She said it over and over,
as if she were Jesus,
and I were dead. She had been
solid as a tree,
a fur around her neck, a
light-skinned matron whose car was parked, who walked on swirling
marble and passed through
brass openings--in 1945.
There was not even a black
elevator operator at Saks.
The saleswoman had brought velvet
leggings to lace me in, and cooed,
as if in service of all grandmothers.
My grandmother had smiled, but not
hungrily, not like my mother
who hated them, but wanted to please,
and they had smiled back, as if
they were wearing wooden collars.
When my leg gave out, my grandmother
dragged me up and held me like God
holds saints by the
roots of the hair. I begged her
to believe I couldn't help it. Stumbling,
her face white
with sweat, she pushed me through the crowd, rushing
away from those eyes

that saw through
her clothes, under
her skin, all the way down
to the transparent
genes confessing.

Naïve Melody

Chris Dombrowski

Some photos I cannot hold without kissing—
this one spilled from the pages of a book
like an aster whose petals, drying there,
infused the words they were pressed between
with a white so vivid the novel's droll
protagonist walked out of his dark midday bar
blinking at a lavish alpine meadow though
it had been December in Flint. A freckle
like a photo is a text the light's helped write
which explains why my friend told the kind
physician that he'd sooner lick the scalpel than
let her scrape six melanomas from his facial
canyons—forty-odd years ago sunlight
prisming on the Adriatic planted those moles
in place, and I can still feel it, he said,
bronzing my cheeks. He knew death was
a wind searching the back of his hand, veins
branching like his childhood sycamore leafed-out
in liver spots, the trunk, its scaly bark, too steep
for memory to climb. But he stared at it anyway
and was somewhere other than that antiseptic
room. Just as I holding this glossy congery
am no longer in the chair where dawn found me
tending my grief in the softening dark. I'm lying
in June grass looking up at her, she's two—
when I go to where he was in those late days
bring me flowers to kiss, hands to press
between pages, bring—Molly laughing, laughing,
Molly with the sun in her mouth.

HOUDINI

Jack Driscoll

So much needless speculation about a key,
how you swallowed it, a silver fish,
and underwater caught it swimming up
between your teeth.
                    That explained
the handcuffs, padlocks, the easy picks
inside that cramped black chest.
What puzzles me is your mother,
how you swore she screamed to you from the grave.
In your dreams she was always drowning
and so you dove from those impossible cliffs,
arms crossed, hugging yourself in a straitjacket.

Except for the crowds, the publicized leaps,
you might have been the escapee
from the small-town asylum, that ward
where men finally fall out of love
with their mothers.
                    You believed one cure
was to make them disappear whenever they walked
barefoot into the bedrooms of their sons, hair down,
asking to be zipped up.

Once, after sleeping late,
the house empty, I stared and stared
at the shape of my mother's lips,
that square of Kleenex almost dissolved, a perfect red O
floating in the toilet.
I don't know why I thought of you, Houdini,
naked beneath the Detroit River.
It was your mother's voice you followed,
her breasts you imagined each time you sucked
those pockets of air under the ice.

That was always your greatest trick,
meeting her in secret while the whole world watched,
inventing easy answers,
not even close to discovering your elaborate deceit.

Snow Bloom

Erin Scott

MILK TRAIN

Stuart Dybek

The barn, whitewashed one morning by snow
and the next by winter fog, disappeared
with the evergreens. What remained
were swaying bells and later a milk train
tugging a delivery of smoke
and a cold front of white refrigerator cars,
a horizon of them crossing invisible pasture
steamed with the breaths of grazing animals
stranded withers-deep in patience,
and after the whistle dissolved,
the wind racing behind along exposed rails
smelled of cinders and cream still grassy
as the hot jet of life spitting from teat
into a ringing metal pail.

SHIPWRECK MUSEUM, WHITEFISH POINT

Nancy Eimers

Here we are with the need
        for another unhappy ending
or at least an explanation
    like light

issuing from the giant Fresnel lens
        now hung from a ceiling
above the faces of the lost
    and their captions of silence

screaming in a gale wind.
        Does the longing to stay alive
ever settle up?
    There are bodies

still down there under the decks,
        up here a dome of heat
has been hanging over half of us
    in this country all week.

Down on the beach
        old trees were flung up
out of the water some old
    ago, roots and all.

Stark, gray, somber, polymorphous,
        they sadden the daylights
out of me. The air so quiet out here
    the lake looks flat

as if it had run out of
        anything more to say.
I wish I could hold a microphone
    to the water;

after that, would trees and their winds
               all seem less scripted then,
more lost
     to reverie?

FELLED

Mary Brodbeck

WHAT IS WRITTEN ON THE LEAVES

Robert Fanning

Of the season, let go. Of the ache to shape and make meaning,
let go. Of the hand in the dark, moss and worm, the awful gnaw.
Of the docked tongue, the root-clenched heart. Let go trunk mold,
branch rot. Of the green shoot that sprouts through your death,
being born, let go. Of quietude, of a peace so deep,
of the changing light—of the euphonious chorus
of children, let go. Of your mother's hand, of your father's laughter.
Of *what has happened to us*. Of all far-flung and gone, let go.
Of holding your head in your hands. Of the sap-drawn kiss,
of the tickle and itch of weeds, of love's ooze and ease, let go.
Of *I am sorry*. Of mote and thorn, of throat dust. Of *I need to,*
I want to, I have to, I forgot to. Of empty and ample. Of all
the threadbare maps, let go. Of lavish and blaze, the crimson
and gold of this glorious leaving. Let go: sister, prayerful sister,
brother hanging from a branch, let go. Of the myriad and ravenous,
these parasitic griefs, let go. Of the gnarled lie, the spine, the trunk
bent earthward, of gravemouth and world. Of *I miss everyone*
even when they're near. Of faith, of the perennial kneel,
of the anchored dream, the hold and hull of flesh and soul.
Of *what should I have said to save you*, of withered stalk: stuck here,
wanting there, let go. Of the clank and drag of anger's black anvil.
Of the fresh and cleansing rain, of every last breath. Of snow,
of the fluttering moth, of the shadow, of the tethers of language, let go.
Of *look at all I've accomplished*. Of province and coastline,
of tall grass swaying, of the thunderhead tumble of summer,
of the loneliness that's known you best, of a box of shells,
of the gulls, let go. Let go of thrust and skirl, of desire.
Let go of panic and skitter and sweat. Of pleasure, of bloodroot
and blossom, of touch and hunger. Of phlox and lily, of homesick,
of *who was I then*, let go. Of marigold, iris, daisy, of the moon
and the pines, of the dew-wet lick and wisp, of the lemon spill
of spring mornings, of chasing kites, of running with shoes untied,
let go. Let go of all the songs. Of wall and beam, of plumb line
and pen, of *I no longer recognize my own hands*. Let go of the worn pages,

of pilgrimage, of grace, of afterward. Of *stay with me, don't go,*
let go. Of all the shatter and ash. Of your daughter's, your son's,
your love's hands, of horizon, of *what will become of all of this.*
Of loose tooth, spindrift, farewell, let go.

[QUESTIONS ABOUT SNAKES]

Lisa Fishman

Questions about snakes were you dreaming
the night-flecked grass and the snake
under the line, under the sheets hung on the line
Were you in the grass barefoot in the night between
one tree
said nothing
heard
A cloud fell down
on the roof of the barn
Was it very many
days like that
Volcano made two boys
pour vinegar over baking soda
every time it was summer and when it was other
flew away

[FROM "CREATURE"]

Lisa Fishman

The silo was falling a stone
at a time, debris at the bottom gathering

Where a door was, rectangle is
In a blue dress the edge

was my body, of the circular
silo standing

BLUE ON BLUE
Nancy Wolfe

INSTRUCTIONS/CONFESSIONS

Lisa Fishman

Then raid the larder of licorice

Then leave the gun where you found it
in the woods behind the house

Then peel off some birch bark
to save for paper and lose it

among the hairpins on your mother's shelf

Then find the accounts of the body
in Anaïs Nin's two volumes

One for pleasure, one for sorrow

Then sing for your supper
down among the willows

wearing many buttons
on your two white blouses

COPPER HARBOR: EARLY OCTOBER

Linda Nemec Foster

Smell of memory and regret and we expect
each leaf, without hesitation,
to engulf itself in its own quiet fire:
the maple turning from light green
to crimson; the oak turning from dark green
to russet. We assume the days grow shorter
and they do, as if to please us, their shadows
lengthening into the forests of pine.

And in the open meadows and low swamps,
the rocky shorelines and wet woods, we know
every wildflower signals its own death—
white of the virgin's bower and boneset,
yellow of the tansy and spotted jewelweed,
red of the Indian paintbrush and cardinal-flower,
purple of the loosestrife and nightshade,
blue of the skullcap and closed gentian,
green of the ragweed and wormwood—
all their colors will effortlessly change
to vague gray before the deep cold begins.

Look at this landscape, the place
that takes nothing for granted.
The sun rises like a sleepy, swollen eye,
while mallards write an uneven calligraphy
on the lake with the short, dark strokes
of their bodies. For them, migration
is calculated chaos: how to get from
point A to point B without dying.

And look at us, with our intense observations,
as if we were spectators that really mattered.
We witness the brief high-color season
when even the weeds enter a state

of self-realization and it stuns us. The hope
that at the end—at the very moment we leave
all that we have become to enter
the coldest of seasons—our colors will be true.

PURPLE SHADOW
Karin Wagner Coron

No Bells in Marquette

Matthew Gavin Frank

In the middle of December,
something rings

in the chokecherry, the bull's eye
of campus, in a blue light

that is three-quarters
at best,

tracks me like a sister
into a world of developing

bells. Husks
pull closed over dying meat.

A dusky tongue gongs
the lips of liberty

and Andromeda is pushed
to the sky's orange rim.

The barntops hide
from the roofs of libraries

and labs, inhabit this season
with humble angles

acute against the night
and the things that sleep

in it. In Palmer,
a television is turned off,

a bed goes dark.
In Republic, a woman checks

to see if a window is closed
because how can this house

be so drafty? Her feet drag
slowly across the carpet

gathering enough electricity
to fill a glass with warm water

from the tap, the faucet
closing like a curtain

in a hospital where
so many babies, just today

were born. Somewhere—
Marquette, maybe—we all

reach an age when we stop
crying over trivial things

and words, where blessings
fall to asphalt and melt.

Under the chokecherry field,
St. Mary's River

hatches its fish in secret,
waiting for the philanthropist

moon to lift
its water up.

STONES AND FOGS
Meridith Ridl

DETROIT

Joy Gaines-Friedler

I once photographed Coleman Young –
twenty years the mayor – he made swearing an art form,
talked in similes, said,

Racism is like high blood pressure,
the person who has it doesn't know he has it
until he drops over with a goddamned stroke.

It was the day my husband moved out
                    and took his power tools with him.

That night a friend offered distraction,
two tickets to Kool and The Gang.

What have the suburbs to offer me now?
The city feels comfortable in my hand.
Like a found rock.

Coleman said, *Courage is one step ahead of fear.*

I think of the sound of factories in the voice
of an old boyfriend from The Cass Corridor –
cocoon of his attic bedroom, mattress on the floor,

candle light and books in that long season of snow
shining in the window – Coleman's city –

Canada faultless in the glass towers along the river.

The word *Renaissance* is painted across this city's
solid surface. The flourish hides its wounds.

TRANQUIL INTERLUDE
Craig Seaver

THE COOL EARTH

Dan Gerber

It's noontime on a summer day sometime around 1948. Boxcars are standing on the tracks, doors open, waiting for the rest of their loads. But it's noontime now and the lift truck drivers are resting. Hay bales stretch out over half the field. The farm hands are resting under the large maple along the fence line, their shirts wet from the morning's hauling, and with the light breeze there in the shade, the rough cotton feels cold against their backs and ribs. I come home, hot from play. My mother has made me an egg salad sandwich, and the screen door waps on its spring. Our dog is resting on the cool earth of the foxhole he's scooped out against the foundation of the house. My father stops to speak to him before he comes in. My father groans as he imagines he would groan if he were the dog, stretching there to his greeting, stiff legged on the cool black earth in the shadow of the kitchen roof. He carries the jacket of his seersucker suit on his arm, and the morning's mail in his hand. There is a knowing, beyond but not apart from this. I hear the *braang* of the spring as it stretches, though there is no slap, as my father eases the door shut behind him. He kisses my mother and drops the mail on the counter. "It's hot," he says, but he clearly enjoys it. He's as happy as I am that it's a hot summer day in our little town and that it's noontime sometime around 1948.

HOLDING

Mary Jo Firth Gillett

for Deborah, in memoriam

The narrow dock shrouded in mist, I can't pick
out even the faintest outline of a boat, let alone
the distant shore. The air's so dense and close
I feel cloud bound, almost afraid to turn
around, barely able to see my own hand
as I nudge the tackle box closer then cast a line

so it arcs away into the grey nothing, line
lost from sight. I can't aim, can't pick
its path of descent, can only wait, my hand
feeling the filament go light as if it alone
connects me to the world. I pivot, turn
slowly, feel the wood beneath my feet so close

I feel it right through my shoes, planks so close
I swear I can sense the grain, the ridges and lines
of growth gone dead. I become landscape as I turn
the reel, slow, cinematic. Virginia, I'd pick
the deep hole near that submerged log. But there's a lone
tug, the tip of the rod bends, and my hand

is a machine at work, fingers little robots, hand
automatic at the reel. Is the world too close
or too far? I fish where water and air merge in a lone
horizon, the place where what appears to be the line
between worlds blurs. I can almost see, almost pick
out small shapes, leaves floating, as fall makes a U-turn

toward ice. Irrepressible, the green oak's turn
from nubby-fingered leaves to these brown hands
adrift on the surface. And as I toy with oblivion, pick
the deep spot, the rod jerks, and I think, so close—

you can be so close to crossing that line
between what's real and not, sane and not, when alone

even you might decide to jump, the lone
thing holding you back, keeping you from a turn
away from reason—the one thing keeping the line
from snapping or going slack—the tension of the hand,
fingers that hold the world lightly, hold it close.
If you're not too tired or too lonely or too sad to care. You pick.

WATERBORNE

Linda Gregerson

1.

The river is largely implicit here, but part
          of what
        becomes it runs from east to west beside

our acre of buckthorn and elm.
          (And part
        of that, which rather weighs on Steven's mind,

appears to have found its way to the basement. Water
          will outwit
        a wall.) It spawns real toads, our little

creek, and widens to a wetland just
          across
        the road, where shelter the newborn

fawns in May. So west among the trafficked fields,
          then south, then
        east, to join the ample Huron on its

curve beneath a one-lane bridge. This bridge
          lacks every
        grace but one, and that a sort of throwback

space for courteous digression:
          your turn,
        mine, no matter how late we are, even

the county engineers were forced to take their road
          off plumb. It's heartening
        to think a river makes some difference.

2.

Apart from all the difference in the world,
                    that is.
            We found my uncle Gordon on the marsh

one day, surveying his new ditch and raining
                    innovative
            curses on the DNR. That's Damn Near

Russia, since you ask. Apparently
                    my uncle
            and the state had had a mild dispute, his

drainage scheme offending some considered
                    larger
            view. His view was that the state could come

and plant the corn itself if it so loved
                    spring mud. The river
            takes its own back, we can barely

reckon fast and slow. When Gordon was a boy
                    they used to load
            the frozen river on a sledge here and

in August eat the heavenly reward—sweet
                    cream—
            of winter's work. A piece of moonlight saved

against the day, he thought. And this is where
                    the Muir boy
            drowned. And this is where I didn't.

3.

Turning of the season, and the counter-
                    turn
            from ever-longer darkness into light,

and look: the river lifts to its lover the sun
                    in eddying
            layers of mist as though

we hadn't irreparably fouled the planet
                    after all.
            My neighbor's favorite spot for bass is just

below the sign that makes his fishing
                    rod illegal,
            you might almost say the sign is half

the point. The vapors draft their languorous ex-
                    curses on
            a liquid page. Better than the moment is

the one it has in mind.

INNER EDGE

David Grath

In Manistee

Mariela Griffor

1. In this city,

they had gardens where the sun rose
face to face with the sand: the sun.
they had an angel of darkness for a brother
they had like all of us
the miracle of life.
They were thirsty and wild like animals
they had like all of us: an emptiness
But at every gesture they made,
a heart was born from their bodies
And, surprised, disappeared into the air.

2. In this city, on the roofs:

Things glisten. The roof is higher
than the clouds. Near to the point of shutting
down the sky out of persistent streets.
And you stand still: between the
Aluminum where the sun fits like a drummer,
completing your life.
Fast swallows threaten
uncontrollable facades.
And you are not there.
The city changes:
the city rolled headlines of tears from the roofs.

3. In this city: like pages of a telephone book:

The newspaper announced today
The city is cutting off all the
Public telephones from
The streets.

The city keeps us inside. It makes images blurry
It settles in cold drops on telephone wires

you go slowly on skis in winter sun
through brush where a few leaves hang on.

They are like pages of a telephone book
with the names eaten by the cold.

In this city, it is beautiful
to hear the hearts pulsing
but the shadows are more real than our bodies.

4. In this city, questions:

To be or not to be
that is the question, right?
with the sky open to so many
God is closer in distance,
but the earth is so populated.

You don't have to be human
to be disturbed,
the animals we eat are disturbed
we flow in between cows and
chickens disturbed by the city:

Women are killed with green
and pink ribbons in their heads.
Man without souls marching
From the past to sit where a fallen
angel sits.

5. In this city, so much effort

So much effort to be a dog
So much effort of the dog to be a dog,
dream in its vigil.
And the daggers dominate,
what moon without stables what nudes,
of flushed, in destructible flesh.
And on the trunk
a boy strains to be a fierce saint
while the saint is
invisible, small with
no strain at all.

FLOATING CITY
Nancy Wolfe

HAIBUN IN NOVEMBER

Robert Haight

It was raining. The fields had been harvested. Now they were brown scalps under a gray cloud. Then there was a lightening, a hint of silver in the sky, streak of sunshine. The raindrops swelled and turned white and feathery in the wind. It was as if a cocoon had burst open and white butterflies had appeared. Or a blanket hatch of September mayflies had erupted on the river. Snowflakes rising and falling, veering in every direction. The field slowly turned white. The trees along the road turned white. The deer hunters couldn't see and left for home to dry out, and the deer moved to the edge of the trees to look out at the field and the snow.

Rain changing to snow
A pick-up truck passed by
Tracks already gone

I live in Detroit

francine j. harris

for Aricka

She said I live in Detroit. And there are no flowers in Detroit.
So why would anyone in Detroit write about flowers in Detroit.

I don't tell her we live under the trees. Root up curbs and dam fire hydrants
to water black pansies licked to the sides of popped black balloons in Detroit.

I'm smashed with the fish under Eastern Market. When the flower vendors
douse cement, I'm the pollen blown off backs of butterflies in Detroit.

Like a lot of flowers, I have split my stem. Cleaved into root balls. Stuck to sweaty
bus windows. Like so much dandelion, I get rinsed down shelter shower drains in Detroit.

There are plenty of violets in flophouses. Pistols broken open
on forty-ounce mouth lids making honeybees bastards in Detroit.

I don't tell her *look around you*. I don't point out the bottoms of coffee cups
where the city spits iris and scratches the back of your throat in Detroit.

I tell her: some of our mothers rescued begonias with cheap plastic planters.
Some of them braided pine into sheets, so we could never sleep again in Detroit.

I wonder if it counts if I wish for frangipani. When I dream in ten spikes of passionflower
to cuff inside my elbow. If I can't leave. Is that enough flower grounded in Detroit.

WINTER ROSE

Erin Scott

WALKING

Jim Harrison

Walking back on a chill morning past Kilmer's Lake
into the first broad gully, down its trough
and over a ridge of poplar, scrub oak, and into
a larger gully, walking into the slow fresh warmth
of midmorning to Spider Lake where I drank
at a small spring remembered from ten years back;
walking northwest two miles where another gully
opened, seeing a stump on a knoll where my father
stood one deer season, and tiring of sleet and cold
burned a pine stump, the snow gathering fire-orange
on a dull day; walking past charred stumps blackened
by the '81 fire to a great hollow stump near a basswood
swale – I sat within it on a November morning
watching deer browse beyond my young range of shotgun
and slug, chest beating hard for killing –
into the edge of a swale waist-high with ferns,
seeing the quick movement of a blue racer,
and thick curl of the snake against a birch log,
a pale blue with nothing of the sky in it,
a fleshy blue, blue of knotted veins in an arm;
walking to Savage's Lake where I ate my bread
and cheese, drank cool lake water, and slept for a while,
dreaming of fire, snake and fish and women in white
linen walking, pinkish warm limbs beneath white linen;
then walking, walking homeward toward Well's Lake,
brain at boil now with heat, afternoon glistening
in yellow heat, dead dun-brown grass, windless,

with all distant things shimmering, grasshoppers, birds
dulled to quietness; walking a log road near a cedar swamp
looking cool with green darkness and whine of mosquitoes,
crow's caw overhead, Cooper's hawk floating singly
in mateless haze; walking dumbly, footsore, cutting
into evening through sumac and blackberry brambles,
onto the lake road, feet sliding in the gravel,
whippoorwills, night birds wakening, stumbling to lake
shore, shedding clothes on sweet moss; walking
into syrupy August moonless dark, water cold, pushing
lily pads aside, walking out into the lake with feet
springing on mucky bottom until the water flows overhead;
sinking again to walk on the bottom then buoyed up,
walking on the surface, moving through beds of reeds,
snakes and frogs moving, to the far edge of the lake
then walking upward over the basswood and alders, the field
of sharp stubble and hay bales, toward the woods,
floating over the bushy crests of hardwoods and tips
of pine, barely touching in miles of rolling heavy dark,
coming to the larger water, there walking along the troughs
of waves folding in upon themselves; walking to an island,
small, narrow, sandy, sparsely wooded, in the middle
of the island in a clump of cedars a small spring
which I enter, sliding far down into a deep cool
dark endless weight of water.

A PRIMER

Bob Hicok

I remember Michigan fondly as the place I go
to be in Michigan. The right hand of America
waving from maps or the left
pressing into clay a mold to take home
from kindergarten to Mother. I lived in Michigan
forty-three years. The state bird
is a chained factory gate. The state flower
is Lake Superior, which sounds egotistical
though it is merely cold and deep as truth.
A Midwesterner can use the word "truth,"
can sincerely use the word "sincere."
In truth the Midwest is not mid or west.
When I go back to Michigan I drive through Ohio.
There is off I-75 in Ohio a mosque, so life
goes corn corn corn mosque, I wave at Islam,
which we're not getting along with
on account of the Towers as I pass.
Then Ohio goes corn corn corn
billboard, goodbye, Islam. You never forget
how to be from Michigan when you're from Michigan.
It's like riding a bike of ice and fly fishing.
The Upper Peninsula is a spare state
in case Michigan goes flat. I live now
in Virginia, which has no backup plan
but is named the same as my mother,
I live in my mother again, which is creepy
but so is what the skin under my chin is doing,
suddenly there's a pouch like marsupials
are needed. The state joy is spring.
"Osiris, we beseech thee, rise and give us baseball"
is how we might sound were we Egyptian in April,
when February hasn't ended. February
is thirteen months long in Michigan.

We are a people who by February
want to kill the sky for being so gray
and angry at us. "What did we do?"
is the state motto. There's a day in May
when we're all tumblers, gymnastics
is everywhere, and daffodils are asked
by young men to be their wives. When a man elopes
with a daffodil, you know where he's from.
In this way I have given you a primer.
Let us all be from somewhere.
Let us tell each other everything we can.

SELF-PORTRAIT AS WATERFALL

Conrad Hilberry

I've been following
this creek bed all my life—
boulders, cattails,

water striders—a thin
meander. When you appear
on the path below,

the cliff gives
into empty air and I fall,
glancing off the limestone,

catching scraps
of sunlight through the sycamores.
Did you know you held

gravity in your hand?
My slow drift
shatters to this broken

light swung sidewise
by the wind. Gathering
myself in a weedy pool,

I offer you two frogs,
three lilies opening into bloom,
and over on that log

a hunched green heron.

KALAMAZOO RIVER SONGLINE
Ladislav Hanka

HUNCH

Conrad Hilberry

Never mind the safe municipal
that claims to offer 3.8%
for fifteen years. Forget

the charts that promise you
the intracoastal channel
when the tide goes out. No

memorizing everything the deck
has dealt. Just follow me
into the tall grass swale

here by the woods. See the way
the sun gets broken
in that patch of swamp?

The way that droop of juniper
makes a doorway
to the dark? Soon you'll hear

the insects' smooth roulette
clicking out your name.
Inside this mound

I carry on my back, some ancient
bones are buried, a trove
where low life stirs,

where larval broods ferment
and generate. Put your hand here
where my humped shoulders

bend to the ground. Feel
the current? That's the fingernail
of luck, crawling up your arm.

STRATA

Mary Brodbeck

DROWN

Dennis Hinrichsen

Fraudulent river, how can
I believe anything you
say? I walk past nine trees, see
a bird, and then that one man
fishing at the edge of vi-
sion is floating by. I can't
see the body at first so
I think his waders are the
trousers of the Lord swelled with
run-off and velocity
from the dam. But they are not.
I don't wade in. The others
with me don't wade in. We just
stroll along, watch the trousers
betray the current through a
flock of un-nerved ducks. It is
only when I call to the
fishermen paddling by to
touch a heel and they recoil
that I sense the heaviness
you carry. Fat man on a
graying Sunday dead of a
busted vein or bubble
in the heart so his body
caved and his garments filled and
he was flannelled thrashing in
waist-deep water. Somebody
must have called from the dam, then
leaned back, fishing. Smoked above
the whirlpools and raw-toothed flail-
ing until the river was

gentle and flat. I am on
the bridge when they pull him out,
so much spilling from his face
I think he is the source of
molten silver. Eyes wide o-
pen. Packed with stone. Because that's
what you are, river, stone lung
and stone heart they try to beat
to life again with useless
hands. Body hauled—such import-
ant fury—from a yellow
rubber boat to the anvil
of a rotted dock I think
a living blade might be forged
fist by fist. My fist if I'd
waded in. My lips two sparks
to ignite a cough. Or what-
ever that stutter is when
the dying gasp and fountain
unrepentant river to
the streaming earth. I wait. No
such breath forthcomes. No such birth.
Just spidery rush-off—ech-
o of a man. How can I
believe anything it says?

Leaving Kalamazoo

Amorak Huey

I am three and there are chickens in the back of this pickup, a makeshift coop. There is rust, and my father plays guitar. I will remember the moment as green, but it is October – already I lie about the small things. We drive south, away from a city of sliced celery, all back yard, above-ground pool, basement. At a stop for gas I find a balloon, unused, this small treasure. It is white, dirty. I am too young to inflate it. I will tell this story for years. Notice how I make myself the hero. Notice how I appear vulnerable while the world sings its blues over my head and the gear shift barks at my knees. Late-day light bends against the highway, and eventually the road turns to dirt. I am not sad we are leaving. Bridges. Rivers. The arc between: a shape no one has named. We are never coming back. I have learned the most important lesson this place offers.

ROUTE 2 HEADING WEST
Karin Wagner Coron

LOOK AT THE PRETTY CLOUDS

Austin Hummell

The most important thing about ice
is that it has no pattern. It takes our children
when they drive home from college for clean clothes
and stuffing, not yet awake to the mythology
of gathering and the beauty of food.
The most important thing about logging trucks
is the whoosh that diverts their attention from the ice
they think is asphalt. After the first whiff
of cedar they hang on and when they look up
it seems like god for a second
has parted the snow with a piece of night.
And that's when they die. The most important thing
about Thanksgiving is that we're always looking
the other way.

               Otherwise we blame the Ice Age
for the Great Lakes and the lakes for letting go
of their water. Otherwise snow is a type of ice
and crystalline a word too fragile for children
to pronounce. It seems cruel to implicate vapor
or the clouds we tested their genius with.
It seems mean that black ice is not black
but transparent, like rime ice, which forms from fog
by trapping the most ephemeral of all things. Children
never last the way we want them to.
The most important thing about the sky
is that it is always there.

ROSE GOLD AND POPPIES

Lizzie Hutton

At 28 I saw that my flat flowered ring had cracked.
    At 35: spring's slaughter house. The old
        stone house, its wild kept food.

They told me it was made of rose gold, how I liked
    the name. *Furred poppy stems and jagged leaves*
        persisting from the white-washed cracks.

That "rose" more real to me than just plain
    gold, although the jewelers told me—
        weeds, they nodded in their place

Their open-faced red heads—that mine was of a type
    once common, inexpensive. *My boy glued there*
        to see the baby pigs released, swell down the hill

To forage on their short blunt freckled legs for fallen nuts.
    A "cigar ring" they called it, made of giant
        sheets of heated gold.

Even so, the sloping pebbled road was beautiful
    at night. The wallpaper designs were rolled on
        in repeating frames. *I couldn't tell, though, if*

Their squeals were greedy grunts or pained—then
    machine-sliced and cut to size, formed into rings
        and put to harden—*even wondered if it was themselves*

They ever ate—like cannoli shells on slender tubes,
    my-finger-shaped. Oh stacks of small mid-whistle mouths,
        lustrous with emotion.

Yet, despite the gold's patrician name—*it didn't matter*
　　to my boy, he held the chain-link, mesmerized
　　　　by the pigs' crowded pink and brown

Coming and going—the ring's flowers were conventional,
　　four-petaled, but for some shut buds,
　　　　their tips pointed like tears.

Now I no longer wear it but I loved it once, I loved
　　the color's melancholy blush and hairline
　　　　crack instead of brass. *The road was beautiful*

At night, sloped, pebbled, rimmed
　　with poppies, wild. And now I knew the way
　　　　I ought to call it. Though I had a boy—

And in the daylight, also, truth be told—
　　a boy who loved the world
　　　　the more for ignorance of all its names.

GOLDEN SUNSET
Michelle Calkins

His 53rd Autumn in Michigan

David L. James

Early November and it comes down to this again: the man sheds, losing his hair, ears, face, a leg dropping in the driveway, his arms torn loose, blown across the yard like fleshy styrofoam. He dissolves into an autumn day, his soul turning that pale shade of sky gray. It happens every year as the evening temps flirt with 30, as trees strip down to scarred bark, as certain birds become memories.

He resigns himself to this fact of living, which is like a fire, bright and consuming at the same time. Thick, cut logs are tossed into the flames; within hours, they're glowing piles of ash, sparking up in a stiff wind.

The man waits for spring when he hopes to reassemble for another year, to piece himself together with what's left from the bitter winter months. This ear is not working well; that arm carries a peculiar ache; his left eye trembles now.

As with every blessing, there's a price to pay.

ON THE EVE OF MY 35TH YEAR OF TEACHING

D.R. James

for Johnny R.

I'm about set to get it right. Go ahead,
call me a romantic constructivist,
and I'll tell you ten years ago
that would have been the insult
I longed to hear. Now I see a wedge
of frenetic ducks following the shoreline
in a V, which if you're trudging north could be
an unstable teepee mutating into an abstract M
that could be a neo-dada W, and I wonder,
Isn't it a little early for this? But ducks
don't know what they're doing, which come
to think of it is just the best metaphor,
since it can stand in for when
I think I do and when I don't know I don't.

I'm on a writing retreat, see—complete with
balmy breezes and solitude, convinced the word
connotes respite, relaxation, and introspection—
when a garbage scow sidles by whose payload
looks like its own mudslide island retreating
into today's flat blue, and I apprehend, again
there's always another way to set things right.

Like my nephew, just received his top-tier Ph.D.
in Education, because of/in spite of which
he's now destitute/astute enough to know
I'll never know and that when classes
begin again next Tuesday, the stiff bailiff
of those new students' anxiety announcing
my auspicious entrance into the judgment
of their lives, I'll be clad in camouflaging
feathers beneath the beat alphabet of my robes.

UNDERGROUND, SOLDER CITY
Mary Whalen

THE SHIVERIN' BITS

Rhoda Janzen

Twilight and evening bell
Alfred, Lord Tennyson

See what happens when you try
not to remember an advertising ditty,
try not to read the billboards placed by
some thoughtful editor in your pretty

margins. You're finally here on Lake Mac
kicking your feet to a distant boat's bell,
watching a pair of focused egrets attack
whatever lies under the water—or, hell,

maybe they're just grooming. The point is,
it's your shoreline, your beach, your neighbor
with the little-boy fountain taking a whiz,
the great reward of all your labor.

The chilled summer sky with its sweater
of clouds was just what you wanted:
the shiverin' bits as you opened your letter
from L.A.; a woody house a little haunted

by a crusty gent in creased serge pants;
to wake up wondering why those tiny lights spin;
to see the water ruffled up with romance
unrelenting as a spicy Harlequin.

It's like a dance with too much liquor—
the billboards roughly tap your shoulder,
so aggressive cutting in that you feel sicker,
such intoxicating vim that you feel older.

And it's not that you're a slow or dreamy dancer.
In the weird half-light the brashest billboards seem
altogether unaware of your new and tender cancer—
Prices Slashed, Jesus Rules, and Try Our Meat Supreme.

Renewal

Jonathan Johnson

This empty Monarch stove and rotting birch aren't much excuse
for my stack of stinking beer bottles. But we do have the snow,

the cars on snowpacked pavement, exhaust in subsequent taillight,
and I want to crack open my fingers, hear nothing

of argument or image, as pure song spills out and fills the room.
Maybe February enters this town with the clarity

of a child's hands, and the lighthouse stands to its knees
in black waves, searching the last cloudbellies before the horizon,

scanning as if some lover might be sailing Superior home tonight,
after all these years. This much alone'd be a sight.

Still, a fine desolation refuses to mix our casualties
with the first blood of the Ironwood girl as she runs

from a barn into a field, twisted junk cars abandoned
like her father's lovers, in the wreckage of the corn.

And if we belong to the Midwest only as abstract
expressionists, it's all the same. We live here

with lake effect piling in our yards. The snow moves through us
without lights and blasts between suspension wires at night

above the Mackinac Bridge, sticking in hundred-foot-tall strands.
And the band covers Pure Prairie League every Thursday, nine to close.

Out at the empty county airport where all the flights are cancelled
blue points strobe in time up the landing strip just in case.

Up in this gable room, the greatest possible bravery
is a hairbrush of yellow spider-web at dawn.

We always toy with hopefulness, splatters
of yellow dot my dark wood floor like dandelions

above all the empty setting, the people living there
under a ceiling of expected snow. Without me,

they sleep. But a few old ones eye the night like crushed food
they can still chew. And shove it in their mouths.

IVAN

Laura Kasischke

Our rooster's name is Ivan.
He rules the world.
He stands on a bucket to assist
the sun in its path
through the sky. He
will not be attending
the funeral, for God

has said to Ivan, You
will never be sick
or senile. I'll
kill you with lightning
or let you drown. Or

I'll simply send
an eagle down
to fetch you when you're done.

So Ivan stands on a bucket
and looks around:

Human
stupidity.
The pitiful
corn flakes in their bowls.
The statues of their fascists.
The insane division of their cells.
The misinterpretations
of their bibles. Their
homely combs—and,

today, absurdly, their
crisp black clothes.

But Ivan keeps his thoughts
to himself, and crows.

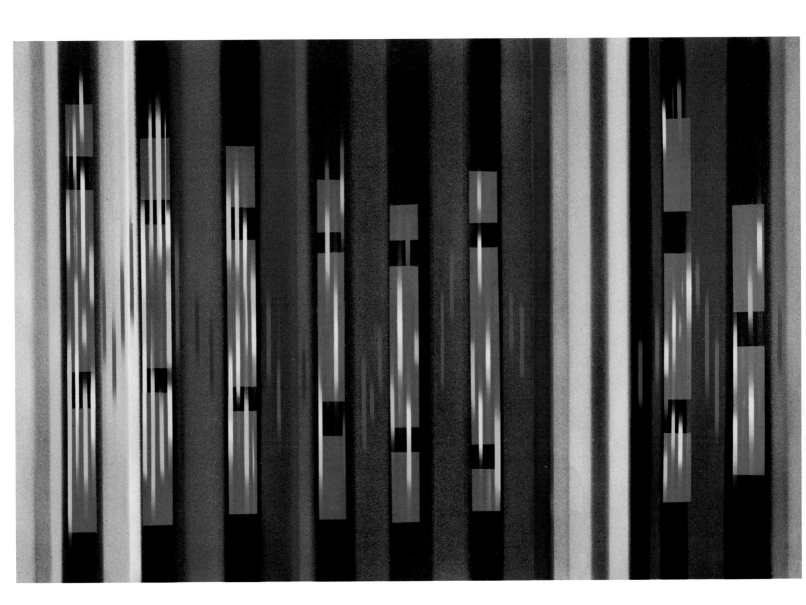

GREEN JAY'S CALL
Carol Hanna

COLD BLUE

Josie Kearns

It was that winter my sister and I
   made the igloo you could die in
      if snowplows worked their teeth just right.

The snow hadn't been stained yet
   with the exhaust of cars, like how
      the moon hadn't been walked on yet

no icicle flag pinning it like a collector's bug.
      I fluffed down in drifts so deep I couldn't
      breathe. The snow had a too-white color, leached

out, the blue of detergent or that new popsicle
   coveted by grade schoolers in 1962 as cool,
      something unprovable as blue-veined flesh

caught in Yukon frostbite, bluegills under
   icy stream. We had heard but doubted that toes
      break off like ice cubes in our frosted metal

trays, that fish eyes harden to coal. I didn't
   understand then, the words: *uncertain*, *sure*.
      I thought maybe this was what blue with cold

meant, some backwards photosynthesis
   or the science of ghosts, but this was before
      cancer melted *his* lungs like blue snowcones

on a heating register, before an embroidered
   tree graced the inside of *her* casket, colder
      than the gown of Pinocchio's blue fairy.

So I kept quiet one whole winter and the next
   not knowing how certain it was
      that cold blue had come into my life.

THREE DEFINITIONS

Elizabeth Kerlikowske

Mourning (v): devouring frozen pizza at every sitting, altering the toppings to track the progress of his escape. Standing before the kitchen window until the smell of burnt crust makes us turn back to the dying room. Eating slowly; gobbling. Our faces keep sliding from the oven baked into expressions of grief which we consume with the intention of it disappearing. Faster until the roofs of our mouths burn, a feeling more appropriate than the squish of casseroles.

Mourning (n): the expression of deep sorrow or numbness by the wearing of black yoga pants and the same too-big sweater three days in a row: our uniforms now and at the hour of his death. His body the sofa that links the furniture in the room. Legs a mottled purple, palms red with liver failure, silvery antimacassar on the arm. The movers cover him carefully with plastic, grateful he is lighter than a piano.

Mourning (adj): a rain-filled mist settling over the wetlands between our eyes and the creek. No amount of rubbing clarifies the scene; the trance of activity including cell phone calls, the traipse of strangers enumerating the stages of the corpse. Sheep comfort at mile marker 54, standing on their straw. Vista at mile marker 48: fruit trees and the bluff facing the big lake. Whole orchards blush as they wake from winter. The vacancy sign in the rearview mirror.

WINTER TREES
Martha Ceccio

ICE FISHING

Judith Kerman

On winter nights,
lanterns scattered across the lakes
chip at the darkness.
Like fireflies, except the season's wrong.
As I drive the back roads,
clumps of trees break up the view:
an inlet, then trees, then another.
Ice shanties hunker down,
haystacks in a dark field.
I've heard that folks
used to move whole houses on skids
across these lakes
with old diesel trucks or 40's Pontiacs.
Maybe it was colder back then, though tonight,
below zero, it's as good as any winter
old people remember.
I can't understand ice fishermen:
walking out
calm as solid earth,
to auger out a hole,
sit on a milk crate hunched over a line
in red and black plaid,
warming their hands
on hot coffee from the Coleman stove,
swigging beer in the shanty with pals
they've fished with since childhood.
Slime and fish scales
on numb hands as they tug the hook loose
from the hard mouth of a fish.
I've handled fish
caught on a canoe trip,
or the koi from my backyard pond,
the body solid thrashing muscle.

I can't imagine walking out on that surface
knowing the void underneath.
Some of them still fish in spring
when the rains come
and water puddles on the ice,
bubbles rise.

Ford

L.S. Klatt

If it's all the same to you, I'd like something more than horsepower. In the 70s, I listened to service tips from a Ford dealer on the radio; it made me anxious to own a Thunderbird, or lose the past in a Galaxie. But when push came to shove, it was a Mazda, Japanese-assembled. Fast-forward to the future, to the yachts of Grand Traverse where Chicagoans from the Gold Coast are insane for our lakefronts. It's true that the high & mighty are mired in foreclosure. You got to feel for the jet set. That puts me in mind of high school when Led Zeppelin ruled the airwaves. Transport is fickle. One of the first Fords, the 999, shot across ice like an arrow but also killed its test driver. Glaciers; they tiptoed interstate with nary an engine.

RETURN OF THE STURGEON
Ladislav Hanka

OLD GROWTH

Kimberly Kolbe

old growth *n.* 1. A long established forest song:
When no one is listening we pray
2. Some woods have been around as long
as God has kept their arms away
from lightning 3. To watch from up above
one's whole life 4. Fastidious holding, i.e.:
What I mean when I say I'll love
you forever is *take me home, Tall Tree.*
adj. 1. The ache in my heart is *old-growth* scar
2. The road home is a shadow, growing
longer than yesterday's love for a fire;
the *old-growth* for a moment flickering—
voc. 1. O, *where will our deep roots hide from the axe?*
2. O, *when will I see a tree and think*—tree?

8,000 Ton Igloo

David Dodd Lee

White it out. I love the sun only because of the clouds. Because they cover me. Because the snow in the winter kills me enough and I can't not be in it. I think of the huge metal hooks and the ropes hardened with ice. Winter in town, in ditches. Cars, giant sharks, and the many nose-dives. The women, the beer. There are fish inside streams that are barely a trickle. There is something about the moon to them, the way they struggle for home, the way they glisten like mail. Then one day you wake to find the trees coated with ice and the dogs wail *For the love of God let me pull something*, and the architecture of reason just falls to pieces. We keep trying to mantle it up. We love, we drink. We try to pull an undertow of logic into the fabric of the day—any day—we find ourselves blessed with, but some of us shoot half our faces off, some drown in the bathtub, some throw the firewood down in the middle of the driveway and just start walking. Eventually a few of us make it to distant southern cities, usually by train, and miraculously there are paying jobs down there, under fluorescent light bulbs, with cigarette breaks and pretty good benefits. But I've seen none of that. I go to the window that is big as a pool table and I watch the stark opalescence of the snow and I can't get it right in my mind, as if whatever there is that's worth dreaming about isn't something you just wake up and find, suffering being somehow different in, say, Texas, than it is here in Michigan, where pain comes draped in silver and silence, and how sometimes you just have to stop whatever you're doing, open a beer, and think about how terrible it is every single day on earth can't be as fucked-up and fine as this one.

BUR OAK AT ANGEL FIELD
Ladislav Hanka

A Dozen Dawn Songs, Plus One

Philip Levine

First the windows gray, then
go black again, but gray is
on the way. Williams lights up
and says, It's on the way, but
I can't hear him over the over-
head cranes. I don't look up
because up is not sunlight
breaking above the eastern
hills or even rain clouds
meant to cool our fevers or
telephone wires clogged with
bad news. Up is the flat steel
ceiling from midnight till now.

#

8 A.M. and we punch out
and leave the place to our betters,
the day-shift jokers who think
they're in for fun. It's still Monday
2,000 miles and fifty years
later and at my back I always
hear Chevy Gear & Axle
grinding the night shift workers
into antiquity.

#

A warm breeze from
nowhere and even the rats scent
the first perfumes of what's
to come, waken, and slide
invisibly into the upper air
to contest the world. Surrender
nothing and never, their motto,

if they have one. They must be
unionized.

#

The river works.
No one flips a switch, no one
shouts "Ready! Set! Go!" no one
writes a memo, it just runs
at its own sweet will its whole
blue-brown length toward five burned
lakes and seven seas.

#

We wait,
the night shift owls, puffing out
our spent breath into the pure air
of 1951. A weak sun not
worth fighting for rises
behind the great brick stacks
of the brewery. War is
everywhere but we don't go because
the streetcar won't come.

#

If I had
a Milky Way I'd share it
with the sparrows picking
about the piss-speckled
snow, if I were reliable and hardy
and had wings I'd pick
about the piss-speckled snow
with the sparrows.

#

              Ragged
flights swarm the upper branches
of the elms only to abandon
their roosts and wheel
across the sky they've wiped
clean, back and forth, back
and forth they wipe until
no clouds or divine signs are left.
Must be some tremor only they
can feel or hawk stink or hint
of human treachery.

              #

              Three mock
oranges do not an orchard make
but will do for now. Light blows
in from Ontario every
which way, hot and cold,
until the owner of the vacant lot
(who also owns the orchard)
kicks off the covers and calls for
sleep and dreams of her, the one
he'll never know.

              #
              Half of us are
women. Think of that! Women,
women alone rising from
single beds meant for sleeping,
women in pairs, women with men
yearning to be free of us,
the men they met last night

or last century. "Give me
liberty or give me liberty,"
their anthem, and they mean it.

One two
three four seconds and Harvey
yells again for Mona to get
her fat ass up. Don't she
know it's Monday workday.
The weekend—the last one, *the*
one—'s long gone and Harvey's
got to have his coffee and his
oatmeal and his lunch box packed
just right, right now.

One two three
four the scuffed black boots down
the stairs. "Does the bitch ever get
anything right?" Slam goes
the outside door, whilst upstairs
the teakettle sirens its answer...
Then quiet, the actual quiet
of public lives in private places.
6:30 A.M., the city of dreams.

There was music. Not
the trite tunes of the blind stars

circling unseen or the gnashed jazz
the trolleys carved
into the avenues or the bad-assed
anthems of the airwaves—
of John Lee, Baby Boy
and Big Maceo—, not even
the music of the immortals,
Bird, Diz, Pres, music of bone
and breast, and breath, music
never heard before. Or again.

#

West
through Toledo, on past Flat Rock
going north. The sign is gone. Leo's
pre-war '39 Chevy four-door
doing its dance routine: a little slide,
a little hold, a little slide on
black ice the devil delivered along
with two bald tires and two good
retreads. The sign's gone, the one
that said "Heaven Ahead" (or was it
Wyandotte?). Sun-up behind us,
last night dissolving in the brine
of light. Coming home one
last time, yes we are!

#

Oh
to be young and strong and dumb
again in Michigan!

DETROIT LANDSCAPE
Stephen Magsig

Save the Frescoes That Are Us

M.L. Liebler

for Edith Parker-Kerouac

These murals would have existed here,
In Detroit, even if Diego had never painted
Them. The sweat and labor of this city,
Along with the sacrificed blood
Of its workers, would have stained
These walls. No matter what.

This town, beautiful, lonely child
Broken by too much post-industrial
Hard luck, is always, once again,
Resurrected with deep convictions.
Our longevity cuts deeper than forever;
It's far longer than Rivera's Lenin-headed
Mural-Rock Center-Manhattan, torn
Down by those city slicker liberals in NYC
Beachhead of American culture and civilization.

Not here! The politics of Detroit
Go beyond arguing fresco vs. classic,
Or any something vs. anything. Here we deal
In a culture of collective energies,
Beating union heart. Here, it's always
Work—Not talk. We know that
Talk is cheap, but work is
Forever. We know
That building is more
Essential to our survival than politics
Is to our reality.

Euclid

Thomas Lynch

What sort of morning was Euclid having
when he first considered parallel lines?
Or that business about how things equal
to the same thing are equal to each other?
Who's to know what the day has in it?
This morning Burt took it into his mind
to make a long bow out of Osage orange
and went on eBay to find the cow horns
from which to fashion the tips of the thing.
You better have something to pass the time
he says, stirring his coffee, smiling.
And Murray is carving a model truck
from a block of walnut he found downstairs.
Whittling away he thinks of the years
he drove between Detroit and Buffalo
delivering parts for General Motors.
Might he have nursed theorems on lines and dots
or the properties of triangles or
the congruence of adjacent angles?
Or clearing customs at Niagara Falls,
arrived at some insight on wholes and parts
or an axiom involving radii
and the making of circles, how distance
from a center point can be both increased
endlessly and endlessly split – a mystery
whereby the local and the global share
the same vexations and geometry?
Possibly this is where God comes into it,
who breathed the common notion of coincidence
into the brain of that Alexandrian

over breakfast twenty-three centuries back,
who glimpsed for a moment that morning the sense
it all made: life, killing time, the elements,
the dots and lines and angles of connection –
an egg's shell opened with a spoon, the sun's
connivance with the moon's decline, Sophia
the maidservant pouring juice; everything,
everything coincides, the arc of memory,
her fine parabolas, the bend of a bow,
the curve of the earth, the turn in the road.

ARCH

Katie Platte

CITY NIGHTS

Naomi Long Madgett

for Gertrude and Eddie

My windows and doors are barred
against the intrusion of thieves.
The neighbors' dogs howl in pain
at the screech of sirens.
There is nothing you can tell me
about the city
I do not know.

On the front porch it is cool and quiet
after the high-pitched panic passes.
The windows across the street gleam
in the dark.
There is a faint suggestion of moon-shadow
above the golden street light.
The grandchildren are asleep upstairs
and we are happy for their presence.

The conversation comes around to Grampa Henry
thrown into the Detroit River by an Indian woman
seeking to save him from the sinking ship.
(Or was he the one who was the African prince
employed to oversee the chained slave cargo,
preventing their rebellion, and for reward
set free?)
The family will never settle it; somebody lost
the history they had so carefully preserved.

Insurance rates are soaring.
It is not safe to walk the streets at night.
The news reports keep telling us the things
they need to say: The case
is hopeless.

But the front porch is cool and quiet.
The neighbors are dark and warm.
The grandchildren are upstairs dreaming
and we are happy for their presence.

AND WINTER

Corey Marks

Au Sable Point Lighthouse, Lake Superior, 1879

1.

When Father opens the door, the storm
is with him, it rushes the dark rooms, flushes
dust from the backs of books and unused chairs.
Down the shore a ship has run aground;
Father's seen it from the tower, a row of lanterns
threading toward us through the rain.

                                        Ready yourself,
he calls, *light the rooms* . . . The gale raves
over his words with its two mouths—wind
and water. Beyond him, the lake rends
its new scars.

                    No home now but this,
Father said in the summer calm
when we arrived, though this is no home.
It is a cage set in the wind.

2.

We have our tasks. Father shrinks into the black
frame of the storm, below the beam
from the hive-shaped lens flailing
the exaggerated night. What choice do we have?
The shipwrecked read a promise in our light
we do not mean.

                     I thought we'd taken residence
at the heart of a refusal that sends the coming world away.
Isn't *that* the vocation he chose for us? Carry the oil
up the narrowing spiral, fill the lamp,
wipe the lens, trim the wick,
set blazing its obstinate *No?*

Autumn arrives with its own commandments.
And winter, which won't stay away—isn't
that the arrival the storm prepares? The edges
seize and the bays close hard
and there is no need to tell anyone not to come
where promise shuts

                its sky-dark door.

Stones That Float

Peter Markus

There are stones along this river's muddy bank that do not sink. They float, though in us brothers' hands, these stones, they feel heavy to us brothers—feel the way that we believe stones should feel: hard, solid, things made from the dirt to be out over the dirt thrown. Throw them into the river, though, and these stones become boats that float on top of the river. Us brothers, we don't know what to believe when we see a thing like this happen. This hasn't always been the way with us brothers and stones. There was a time when, us brothers, we remember stones that used to sink. We'd throw them up and above and into the river and watch them disappear. In the darkness of the river we'd hear these stones go plunk and plunk. Maybe now it's the river and not the stones. Maybe it's that the river is more mud than it is water now, and the stones that we are throwing aren't really floating. Maybe what these stones are doing is, they are just sitting there the way that stones sometimes sit in the mud: sit, and sit, for years, for centuries, until us brothers come walking up and along the river's muddy shore and reach down with our muddy boy hands to pick the stones up from the mud. We pick the stones up from the mud so that we can throw them, so we can see a stone in flight, can stand and watch this thing without any wings rise above this earth.

JAZZMAN

Nancy Wolfe

AN OCCASIONAL POEM

Dave Marlatt

You all know very well that
marriage is a train ride
from Chicago to Los Angeles on the Super Chief.
You wake up in Oklahoma City in the afternoon.
Count Basie and Oscar Peterson are playing
dual pianos in the club car. Jackie Gleason's
behind the bar wearing a black leather bow tie.
He's just dropped two olives into the martinis
he's making just for you.
Listen carefully. The two women in the red vinyl
and chrome booth across the aisle are talking about you.
Yes, the two of you.
It's Carole Lombard and Greta Garbo.
They're wearing some kind of matching skin-tight
rose-colored satin dresses that seem inappropriate
in the afternoon sun although altogether irresistible.
Carole says what a lovely couple you make,
wishes she were on her own honeymoon and
tells you what Clark Gable is really
like in 25 words or less.
Before she can finish, Ernest Hemmingway sideswipes
your table. Invites you to Ketchum to shoot
birds with Gary Cooper
to make up for spilling your drinks.
This is just all too irresistible.
Suddenly there's a commotion in the smoking car.
Several white-jacketed waiters rush back through
the door where you can just see Frank Sinatra's fist
wrapped tightly around Ava Gardner's wrist.

I've heard of successful marriages being accompanied
by the sound of the bowling alley next door, the infinite cacophony
of falling pins and cranking machinery. Inside
behind the lanes, you know all the self-medicating
bowlers, and every night, someone known or unknown
comes home drunk every hour on the hour
making a racket, looking for the light switch.

Some marriages are accompanied by the sound
of my grandmother vacuuming under the dining room
table at 4:30 in the morning.
She can't sleep, so why should you.
And it's not altogether unpleasant.
By 6:30 she wipes her hand on the front of her apron
calls the two of you downstairs
into the kitchen before your eggs and bacon get cold.
She can make the dogs across the street begin to howl.

Occasionally, I hear heavily loaded freight cars heading North,
that low nearly imperceptible shudder of ground
as it sounds over 119th street where there's
no crossing gate. I listen as if it were the sleek streamlined
Super Chief, a sound I've heard before
over a rolling sea of grass
far away and reliably distinct.

I Don't Want to Say How Lost I've Been

Gail Martin

Missed my road by Cathead Point, took the wrong loop on the trail at Port Oneida. Got so turned around on Voice Road by North Bar Lake I couldn't speak for three days. I went to the IGA after it closed. Good Harbor Grill doesn't serve dinner. I never know which side of the road the river will be on. It takes me a while to realize I'm lost. You could call that confidence or part of the problem. Lake = north, lake = north, I say to myself, but lake = west and northwest a bit down the road, and there's a lake to the east here too. A friend's husband draws a map by hand each time she leaves, CANADA at the top, MEXICO at the bottom. The oceans are implied. This is to help her know if she overshoots a turn. I understand. I love maps, the names, the blue shapes of lakes and rivers. I can find my way anywhere theoretically. What's hard is the YOU ARE HERE part. And it isn't exactly loneliness, although I'm calling it that.

BLUE BARN, SUPERIOR TOWNSHIP
Karin Wagner Coron

SLEEPING BEAR

Kathleen McGookey

I climb the dune's highest hill. I want to fly away home. Up here, it's quiet and breezy. Slowly, a toy boat draws a white line across Glen Lake. My heart calms. The people who climb after me have not hurt each other. Campers stream off a blue schoolbus, then wobble in canoes near shore. Though I know they must be singing, I can't hear the song.

FIRST SNOW

Judith Minty

I love this meadow with all the weeds erased,
this stunned silence
with no house in sight, everything soft
as chimney smoke, as the breath steaming out of my mouth.
When we were children in the city, we'd count
star-points on snowflakes, then lick them off our mittens.
We loved what was cold then, loved
the feel of change in our bodies.

Now I live in the country, just this old black dog
for a friend, and we're on our way to the mailbox
—it's the same path we've traveled through summer and fall,
only this time our steps creak on fresh-fallen snow.
Past the curve of the drive is the road to town,
but I'm watching the dog prance along beside me,
I'm listening to chickadees in the pine tree in the hollow,
I'm counting all the blizzards and thaws I've spent here.

The dog stops to sniff where a rabbit has paused
and the world seems poised on its axis.
Coming back, her nose will record that we've passed here,
I'll be holding white envelopes with their own trail to follow.
—But now, we're here. We haven't reached the road.
Now the chickadees explode from the pine in a clamor
and the dog turns to me and she looks like she's grinning.
Now she throws herself down on the snow, she rolls
onto her back, she spreads out her wings.
I think I see ghosts in the birch grove up the hill.
I'm talking to my dear ones in heaven.

VACATIONLAND

Ander Monson

This place, this bearer of the chilly winter burst,
the white-out everywhere and flurry,
the not-in-the-terms-of-Dairy-Queen,
this blizzard with a lowercase *b*,
far from commercial in its constancy,
its threat, impact, and our recovery:
always from it. We are always re-shoveling
out the driveways and panking down the snow
or breaking up the ice with handmade iron spears
or spokes wrested from bikes that have succumbed
at last to rust. This is my vacationland, my very own
Misery Bay, my dredge, my lighthouses, my vanishing
animal tracks in snow. Everyone who is not from here
is *not from here*, and that is all there is to say.
Everyone from here is still from here
regardless of where they are or where they end.

White light filtering through snow like dust.
There is always light coming down
like a donation from God—a little perk
to get us through the winter. This light
lights up our faces, lights up the faces
of the frozen dead as seen on TV from Canada.

This vacationland, this motel open year-round,
is now a Best Western and that is good, I guess.
This vacationland, this Michigan,
my Michigan, is no destination, no getaway
for us, those who are always *from*.
We have no destinations. We have no way
to get away from her, from here, to get away
from romantic winter getaways and those
who've come to get away from their dull bombs of city lives.

We cannot get away from *from* and from the doldrum
winter silent burn. We might as well be stone—agates,
mottled trifles, appearing periodically on the beach
to be taken home, to be put with other pretty rocks
and bits of lake glass in jars. We are meant for your mantel
and for the light that will find us there.

We might as well be the kind of rock
that passes for rock on the radio up here,
meaning Foreigner and Journey and nothing
that could be ever meaningful again
because it has been subsumed by soft-rock
crap-rock, classic-rock, by radio, by frequency-
modulated energy in air, by the tyranny
of awful playlists and shitty DJs
and no hope of getting a decent song
played for us to be indifferent to at prom.

We are what is left. We are drift.
I guess this is a sort of manifesto.

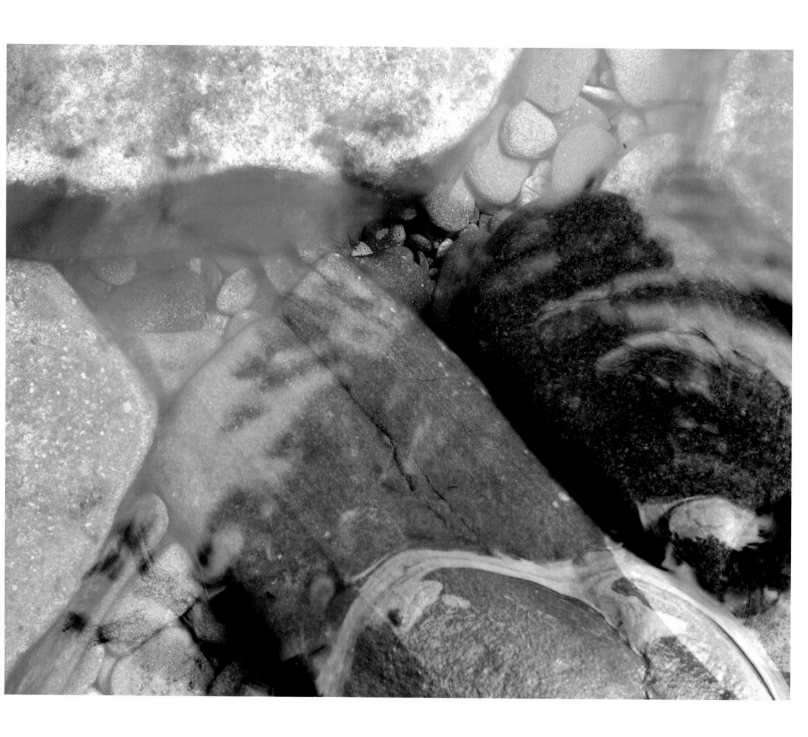

WATER ROCKS

Steve Coron

RENOIR'S BATHERS

Julie Moulds

What is it about women in water
that almost makes them part of the landscape?
Renoir's bathers, pink and mustard
and vaguely nippled; their ample thighs
rising from a purple river in a scene
centered by one brown tree. What is it
about women, painted by men,
that they become landscapes, creamy roses
in a garden? In another age,
when people could still sleep
with almost anyone, my sister and I dipped
ourselves naked in a Michigan lake, both of us,
still, miraculously, virgins.
I suppose some painter in that art colony
where Brenda washed dishes
could have captured us, like Renoir,
two flowers with leafy thighs and brown
daisy faces. Perhaps he would accent
our round hymens with petals. I want to be
the woman, with her brush, sitting in an oak
above a pond where twelve nude men are frolicking.
She is painting a landscape of men:
lying flat with grapes above their open mouths;
men, with buttocks turned towards her; men,
with arms arched behind their long necks.
She would call it *The Dozen Adonae*. Pink
chrysanthemum men; dark, magnolia men;
legs spread, organs rising or fallen,
depending on your eyes. In another time,
in a deserted field, I lay naked as a lover
wrapped me in oil. I must have even walked
through high grass, and, knowing me, worried
about where bugs could enter.

Insects never crawl up the legs
in the paintings of the three Graces.
In those landscapes of the masculine
dream, men want to paint us perfect,
from a distance, then break petals,
like a cloud or a swan.

IN THE NEW ORCHARD

Amy Newday

It started with the peppers my mother ate
all summer the year I was conceived, peppers
from the side garden across the driveway

and whatever else grew there. Was it her first
garden since childhood? Peppers, and probably
beans, cucumbers, tomatoes. My mother drank

cows' milk straight from the bulk tank and I
drank hers. Sunlight dropped through space
onto the hillside above the garden where cows

stretched out long tongues to pull it
into their mouths. It started with that sunlight
and that grass and later I'd eat their bodies,

I'd scrape my teeth across the marrow
of their bones, I'd race the path along
the fenceline of wild mulberries,

through a thicket of weeds, through a frenzy
of bees, cows crowded the corner shade,
I could hear water running underground—

I had a body! After frost now, apples roll down
the tree-studded lawn where the mulberries
used to be. Gone the hummocked manure,

the burrows of woodchucks humped
and sandy, my little shelf on the wide branch
where I kept books wrapped in plastic,

where I hovered over sadness and lilies
of the valley made an elfin grove below me.
Mouthfuls of berries, sweet and black.

I remember I cried when they bulldozed
those trees—flayed and stripped and sawed—
but to want them back now would be to want

Indians riding out of the swamp
like Jesus on his donkey, waving feathers
or red handkerchiefs, to resurrect

the gospel of this ground already inside
me. I may as well want a field of hail-
scorched wheat, a sunset or a vanished

language, I might as well wait for hell
on earth, for my own body to fly
from this robin's nest baptized

in the new, improved, chemical
rain. Instead I dip my hands between
yellow leaves and eat hardy kiwis—

plump, purple-rouged green, grape-sized,
clustered, unlike tropical kiwis, their smooth
skins split between my teeth. I don't wait

to wash them, though I know the gray flecks
are guthion, which triggers a little machine
gun in the brain, neurons firing, firing, firing.

Birch and Pine Trees, Northern Michigan, 2012
Nathan Caplan

LEAFDOM

William Olsen

These leaves are neither poems nor Whitman's hair.
Scuttling across sidewalk openly, whatever they mean.

No scented handkerchief, no hair of young men.
Nor of women, daughters or sons. Nothing ours.

The world below is where these leaves return.
They've fallen, and the ground is their heaven.

I have been there and you have and that's where
Our fathers and mothers came from, and their ancestors.

From earth the stars rise, and quiet human gaze.
The stars come up like trees.   They quiet words.

The leaves are not blood let of innocent childhood:
I can get over these leaves.   Their deepening mess.

I can read practically anything into these leaves.
But the isolate beauty of doing so can feel awful.

They have nothing to do with books or book-burning
Or Kindle or freedom fetishized by technology.

They don't know the summers are getting longer.
They have no idea. They can't even imagine us.

I could blame myself, but I'm not sure, that sounds
Beneath human decency and beside the point.

I could fault the passage of time, but I'm not sure
I could find a God to believe in me. And I could

Go on taking these walks until these walks stop.
Life is unfair. That life is unfair is unacceptable.

That's the dumbfounded prayer behind poetry.

Kalamazoo, October 2010

GOOD

Anne-Marie Oomen

Against swirls of winter chores, shoveling grunts,
    wind-driven winter, the woman
        decides to do some good.
She knows the pregnant cat will birth.

She dreads the starved waifs in the milking barn,
    cold mewing on her back step,
        snarling dead run for house scraps
when all their mouse hunting is done,

and there is nothing left. There is nothing left.
    They will bloat as they starve, ornamented
        with frostbitten ears. She scratches
at her dry hands. She hates the look

the mom-cat takes when the warring litter clings
    to her teats. That utter stupidity.
        She hates the way men kick
them aside, tie their tails, hang them from nails.

Before the mom-cat can lick them clean,
    before her own kids find them,
        before anyone could grab her sleeve,
her knee and beg for, oh, anything more from her,

before she wonders what is good—
    what makes good, what is God
        who makes life good, she knows this:
make no mess, leave no trace.

Sweep the slick packages into a cherry pail
    filled with icy well-water—oh,
        necklace of little moons bubbling—
until everything is still, as good as she can make it.

FOREST

Miriam Pederson

Color has drawn him into the maze
of the Hiawatha Forest.
It is hunting season,
but he doesn't know it yet.
Maple leaves tick
as they touch the forest floor;
a roar is in the oaks
whose fullness speaks to him
of hanging on despite the wind,
despite the song of letting go.
Past the hardwoods
and into the evergreen mass he forges.
Gun shots clear, almost rhythmic now,
and he's conscious of the time of year—
the month, the day, his memory allows.
Soft needles cushion his footsteps.
He tries to whistle, to hum
and then to sing aloud
because he's lost and afraid
to be mistaken.
I am a human being,
he starts to chant
loud as fluorescent orange, he hopes,
I am a human being—
and he laughs between
each triumphant declaration—
not crazy yet,
just finding the words
he's needed to say for years.

LONG LEGGED FOX
Tom Walsh

Neruda in Kalamazoo

Susan Blackwell Ramsey

Neruda shakes his head at Kalamazoo,
    but he's half-amused. There, in the corner
of Water Street Coffee Joint, in the flat cap,
    watching from under heavy lids with eyes
darker than the espresso he hasn't tasted.
    He's working on a metaphor equating
a nation's eros and its taste in coffee.

He isn't optimistic. Watching the slender,
    bundled young ordering their syrups, soy milk,
(*blood of anemic beans*, he mutters,) he worries
    for them. Such dilute fuel for love with all
those layers of wool, down, fleece to penetrate.
    He sighs. Even their pale eyes afford no traction,
strike no sparks. It's like wrestling water.

But as he shakes his head, he sniffs, looks up.
    Cinnamon. A girl at the counter is sprinkling
cinnamon straight into her coffee cup.
    The young man at the table to his left
forms a fist under the table. Outside
    the gravel is resolving into mud.
Well. Perhaps. He opens his paper, sips.

THOUSAND DOLLAR DAYS

Greg Rappleye

The man at the picnic table
in front of the root beer stand
in northern Michigan is my father.
Do you see his sign,
twirling through the piney air?
There are two hours until he opens,
and he's drinking a cup of black coffee,
making a list for the salesman
from the wholesale grocery,
who'll be banging at the back door
after the noontime rush. The sun
angles from the gas station and across
the parking lot,
where crows compete for popcorn
dropped by last night's customers,
mostly teenaged kids,
on vacation with their parents
from the suburbs of Detroit.
It's the summer after the summer
their city burned. Martin is dead and Bobby is
dead, and Nixon is yet to come.
Denny McLain is flaming his way to 31 wins,
and America thrashes in the bed
of Southeast Asia. But in a tourist town,
traffic is what matters.
So my father lays his pen down
to watch the passing cars, subtracting out
the junky Fords and pickups of the locals.
Inside, the hired woman wipes a rag along the counter
and begins to sing a hymn,
her voice carrying through the screens
and rolling sweetly below the canopy
that shelters as many as fourteen cars

on rainy afternoons. My father's eyes
are gin-clear, and he's sketching out plans
to add barbecue after the Fourth of July.
He counts three good car hops,
four sons and two daughters,
old enough to hold their own
through the heaviest dinner hour.
The season hasn't really begun,
but already he's had thousand dollar days.
My father smiles. His lot is
full, he imagines the rush,
as his hand strikes something
from his list. And I'm the skinny boy
you see, legs furiously churning,
rounding the corner from the old highway
to the new, sprinting toward the pylon
that rises from that one-story building
like a jagged orange fin, who sees his father smiling
and believes, against all the evidence,
that he might be the reason why.

New Mott Hospital from Mitchell Field

Steve Gilzow

THE NIGHT THE TIGERS BEAT THE YANKEES

Josh Rathkamp

All I saw was one member of Earth
Wind and Fire playing backup guitar
with a lead singer just good enough
to keep me there,
paying ten dollars a beer
while the slot machines and craps tables
rolled on without me.

If I wasn't almost broke,
wasn't still pissed at my poor job
playing cards, I would have been happy
as the man in a floral shirt
who handed me a Bud Light
and clinked the bottom of our bottles
when he said *cheers*.

I wanted to cheer, to go back
to Detroit in '84
where cars still got built
by American hands, by American parts,
by men in town
who proudly bought and drove them.

Even on Saturdays garage doors rose,
headlights turned the corner and vanished.

So my dad was the only dad left
steering the van to the game.
We'd pile in the back, drive downtown,
see the buildings that cars made,
the large steel towers before
the broken windows, the houses
before they were shut up by boards.

We'd pass Grand River and Woodward,
streets as forgettable as the reason for their names,
how men rode north
into this great gray state
and sent logs down the rivers, so many
you could walk straight across without falling through.

AT SWAY

Christine Rhein

Before air conditioning, the city sidewalks
alive with hopscotch, two-square,

monkey in the middle, with grown-ups
hurrying to the store or the bus stop,

I used to sway on daisied vinyl cushions,
an old metal glider that had somehow—

like our renter—come with the house,
glider I loved as much as the front porch,

a covered, roosted room open
to leaves and dragonflies and breeze,

to the sounds of neighbors, of parents,
fights and, sometimes, laughter,

sometimes rain—magical to stay dry,
suddenly cool with storm all around,

rumbles and crashes, the wet smell
of the world, water flooding gutters

and curbs, plunging everywhere at once,
like my heart at all it longed to know—

the questions themselves, balls thrown
just above my head, beyond my reach...

Today, in the frost of middle age,
I drive back and forth—the first time

in thirty years—on the street of my youth,
trying hard to recognize the few houses

that haven't been demolished, the treeless
lots, and wondering what I might be

looking for in the spot—grown so small—
where the porch must have stood,

where the sweet creak of the glider
has turned to *then, now, then, now.*

Mermaid Blue, from "A Night Sonnet, So Far"
Mary Whalen

It's April and It Should Be Spring

Jack Ridl

The gods are tired of tending fires.
Against the window, a cold rain.

Each night the hour hand moves
time and us closer to the light.

No one wants to go out. No one
wants to stay in. And the rain.

Robins do their silly walks across the lawn,
dead grass dangling from their beaks.

Crocuses raise their purple risk
through the ice-crusted mulch of maple,

oak, beech, and willow. They last
a day. Clumps of daffodils stay

blossom-tight. We want to put away
sweaters. What would the saints do?

We haul in more wood. It is raining.
Sunday and it is raining. And it is cold.

Winter's wedged itself into a crack
along the equinox. We know, in time,

the trees will bud, the flowers rise
and bloom. We do what the earth does.

THE UNEMPLOYMENT IN PALMER

Ron Riekki

taps me on the shoulder
and by taps me I mean
shatters my collarbone.

I can't really see anyone
in my family with a job,
which means I'm blind

as a bat, and here I'm
talking about a baseball
bat, no eyes, no ability

to see—and not used
for a ball game but used
to crack over the skull

of someone with a gambling
addiction, who sits at the edge
of the dock and doesn't realize

that he's sitting on more
than one edge and everything
slowly keeps creeping up.

ROCK SHORES

Meridith Ridl

THREE LANTERNS

John Rybicki

There's our son at the end of my hook
    riding over the Detroit River

where Tecumseh's still rowing
    towards his oblivion.

This boy we're casting to the land
    of the leaping frogs.

My lass lives on the floor
    where the fish are frying,

her spine snapped in half
    the way a Milky Way might.

She squares her thumbs and fingers together,
    frames for our son

a picture window to climb through.

          *

Eighteen months with us
    and our dark-skinned son

still has pockets sewn over his clothes.
    They're filled with stones

that keep a boy underwater,
    his vowels bubbling up to us.

With our brooms and hockey sticks,
    we're swatting away

city streetlights that followed him here,
 those bulbs that bow

and peck at his back.

*

My love's trying to stop the chiming,
 her fingers so singular

since that one dark bell of cancer
 is ringing again in her neck.

I hollow this house while she sleeps,
 take my time and chisel

the proper curve so our canoe
 cuts easy through rough water.

My lass is a sweet tomahawk
 for the scalping

of moons and runaway boys.

*

We hold hands over our son's
 mouth when he sleeps

so his body blows up and floats.
 We nail our stakes in the yard

to keep him
 tethered to this world.

See how he splashes
    in summer when he knocks

his mouth against moon water.
    See how we paint with one finger

bright horses across his ribs,
    and rivers on the outside

streaming down his arms.

*

Sometimes we sketch with smoke
    a door just over

that rock in our boy's chest. You can hear it
    rusty when he knocks

on our bedroom door to tell us
    he's been throwing up

for two months now
    like he saw his blood mom do.

We take the scent that falls from him –
    baby powder, gunpowder –

into our skulls because we live
    in an empty house,

and in each bedroom there's a bell
    ringing under the covers

where a child might live.

We sledge the stake in our yard,
    then let the line out slowly

until our son's way up there
    where the moon makes

a lovely mess of him.
    When my wife and I

are overwhelmed with this,
    we beat our skulls upon the moon,

and it empties over the earth.
    I tell you, when we kiss,

even the little bell in my love's neck
    jingles, it rhythms,

it makes a lovely sound.

DIA Window

Jean Canavan

AT GLEN LAKE VS. THE BIRTH OF ANGER

Mary Ann Samyn

Briefly put, I was spring-fed,
like many a lake.

For his part, Jesus slept a lot,
while others worried.

Returning home isn't easy;
no one said it would be.

Talk about comfort zones,
sticky sadness—

The children drew chalk crucifixes,
two versions; please vote.

All around the lake, tiki lights mean
someone's making a party.

Good for him is what I thought;
I'll pray to that.

My Life in Heaven

Mary Ann Samyn

This is a true account beginning now.

Here's a birch basket, tens of feathers, none of which will ever belong again.

This is like that, only more so.

Once I was a little girl who tried to write it.

Now I do twenty years' worth of looking every afternoon.

Like the insect that shed its *before* on the sand, and unstuck its wings, two pairs.

Time can't be wasted; some changes are forever.

The lake's three greens know, and its darker churning, and its eyelet edge.

Given the chance, I'd wear that to meet you.

JULY FOURTH

Teresa Scollon

for my father

One year ago today you rode in the village parade
at the invitation of the friend who sat beside you:
a stiff-legged farmer dressed as the Easter Bunny—
his costume as randomly strange

as everything else that was happening to you.
I watched you from the curb. You were waving
and waving, grinning, your face still rosy,
your scalp balding under the campaign hat.

You'd retired from office before you got sick
but he'd asked you to dress as Mr. America,
so you dug out your campaign posters,
bright red with bone-white letters.

We'd agreed it'd be good for the town to see
you. Stories had you half buried already,
and we were all so broken, panicked
but not saying so. And you relished the joke

of a sick man running for office, so Irish
in its blackness—nothing funnier than disaster.
And it *was* funny, you in the street before us, smiling,
leaning out of the little rig as if about to spring

into conversation with us. How you loved to laugh
and greet people—that ritual and talent of mammals:
greeting—and you were so good at it, rolling in
with a grin and a little crack, laughing

at yourself and this comic predicament,
this terror, we share. And we loved you
for it. People still talk about your smile.
Here in our town on July Fourth, it was good

for us to see you. It was good for you to hear us
calling to you. It was good for all of us
to smile and wave and heal each other
for that mile and a half of public sun.

WOMAN IN GREEN, FROM "A NIGHT SONNET, SO FAR"
Mary Whalen

Sleeping Woman

Herbert Scott

after the painting by Richard Diebenkorn

I'm walking east down Lovell in Kalamazoo
in the middle of the afternoon, and it's hot, July
something, and there's a man sleeping on the sidewalk—
the way you would in your bed—his body a kind of Z
in a fancy serif font, the curlicue of hands
beneath his head at the top, and the toes of each foot
curved to comfort the other, at the bottom. At first
I don't know if he's alive or dead, his skin
the color of burnt iron, a darkness alcohol finally brings.
I remember him from months before, a couple of blocks
west of here. He leaned against my car and wanted
to borrow money, a loan. He wanted a ride to South Haven
where he could get the money to pay me back.
His voice had that desperate familiarity that says:
You know me. You must want to care for me.
I think I gave him something, not much, and drove away.
I couldn't forget his face, murky with solitude,
like the hard red clay in Oklahoma where I grew up
that won't grow anything—everything lost to erosion
that brings such desolation you can't survive.
I thought he wouldn't survive more than a week or so,
but here he is, and when the cops arrive they know him,
call him Billy, and he's still alive, maybe
for the last time, and they pick him up.
I head east again, turn left into the cool museum
where I lose myself, sometimes, where I find you
sleeping where I've seen you before, paint streaming
around you like water, gathering in the shallows
of your dress. I am always surprised to see you.
I don't know. Are you flesh, or water? If I move
you will disappear in a startle of color.

The gallery is almost dark—those new-fangled spots
that keep the viewer anonymous—but your face turns
toward me from the crook of your doubled arms,
all about you an unencumbered sway, an intelligence
of light explicit as a summer evening. Deer quietly chewing.
I balance, in the shadows, between.

Snowstorm on Mozart's Birthday

Herbert Scott

Kalamazoo, Michigan

The teachers of winter
let down their long hair.

We lie back on our beds
and disappear
in the pale, quiet muslin.

Twenty-seven inches of snow,
and Mozart on the radio.

The neighbors are pushing
through five-foot swells of snow.
Where will they go?

The city is adrift,
but Mozart on the radio.

Mozart, we are thankful.
The air glistens with music
and we lie back again and again.

The sky flings down its lovely notes.
Mozart on the radio.

GRASSY MICHIGAN CENTRAL STATION
Alanna Pfeffer

BALLET AT MIDLIFE

Heather Sellers

In a strip mall off the highway,
cased in black tights, under fluorescent lights,
five women twist toward the window, arms aloft,
wavering, waving, as though saying *hello, stop!* Unbalanced
at the *barre*, we are stranded, flocked—it's a squeeze,
on tiptoe, a shot at the last shot we've had since
we were girls: beauty. Or flight? Or is this weird
workout simply a way into *body*, a final attempt to be
in love with and not fighting *body*? I always forget
an elastic to hold a ponytail. I'm the dark one
on the far end, behind long curtains of dark (dyed) hair.
The one not afraid to look in the mirror. I'm curious,
like a new world explorer reading a map:
what *are* the head lettuce lumps stuck
onto the sides of my hips for? Why does my butt
look like two ships? Where is any of this produce,
voyaging headed? And Patricia, beautiful, thin, ancient, flanges,
singularly, disastrously, unable to hear the beat.
Any beat—she doesn't associate movement
with music or her heart. This is Ballet One.
An ongoing class. I kick her, she says sorry,
pas de bereft, pas de moronic; *plie*, flee-ay.
And we're down on the musky mats.
My back arches on command (I miss
sex.) (I miss jump rope.) (I miss live music in
smoky backwoods North Florida juke joints, longnecks
and Slut Boys, dancing like rubber wire.) The fit little teacher
struts past with her stick named Stephanie the Stick.
Press it! Press it! Five six seven eight. It's late.
Ladies, ladies! We're the ladies, somehow the ladies.
We walk our feet out. We thrust pelvic
bones up, bridge higher, higher. Doorknobs!
Bowls! We hang from the girlbone.
What isn't written here on this ridge?

Some uncertain, lonely god, some minor
new god looking for a project in a minor key could
drive by the strip mall cosmetology college,
The Barking Lot (dog day care), past Dos
Hermanos and New Again Used Things,
and see these lycra-balded bones, our roots,
chin hairs, Dolores's hammertoes, Marie's
fused spine, the balletic barge fleet, and see
instead of thin carpet over the cement foundation,
a green still lake, the choreography of fierce
splendid living—pale feathered bodies listing
and living fiercer for the not-flying. Not sinking.
Not floating. Not swanish. Swanish. Alive.
Thursday nights from five to six P.M.

DON'T FILL THE OUTLINE

Diane Seuss

the hound left behind with a hound. You
know how good it can be, holding an empty
leash. When the fire station burned it was

a relief. No red truck to shine, no bell to clang,
no hose to wind up or unwind. Admit you know
how pretty it was when Ellie gave birth to a moon

out on Born Street behind the hog market, that kid
without a face, its head just a bare bulb, a circle,
silvery, like a hand mirror. You know when a tooth

falls out, the gap gives your tongue something to do,
that when the mushroom factory left town there was
no more manure in the wind all summer. Remember

when Simplicity shut its doors, how renegade
dress patterns went blowing down the alleys
and fluttered like paper birds in the limbs of trees?

EMPIRE

Mary Brodbeck

DRIVING LESSONS

Patty Seyburn

No parking lot with orange, immaterial
cones, we ventured forth on the feeder roads
of I-10, the John C. Lodge (so dubbed for a
dead big-*macher*), highway that siphons off
its denizens to every self-determined corner
of the Motor City. Emblems of identity
borrowed from myth and literature 101,

Rochester, Romeo,
Royal Oak, Romulus

Chippewa, Ojibway,
Ottawa, Huron

pillaged from natives or merely descriptive:
here's what some buck-skinned boy who
thwacked a wilderness path first saw in
the clearing—if he didn't name it for himself.

My family's last name borrowed from
the upper-crust, and they'd never know that
a Jew from Toronto adapted their assignation,
clean and British, someone born at sea in the
caste-driven past, or that their namesake would
don a white shirt with rolled-up sleeves, draft
and check fine lead-lines in service of that
noble democratist, Henry Ford, creating
"a car for the great multitudes." And when
he asked Marianne Moore for names did their
lyrical excess turn his head toward "Edsel,"
notorious flop? These were not words for
the multitudes, he thought. The name changes
the named and its purpose.

Mongoose Civique,
Turcotingo, Utopian
Turtletop, Magigravue

Know when to speak out, when to fit in.
I spun my web of unobtrusiveness, learned to
laugh derisively at crash-test dummies'
demise in cars with fins older than we were
and gentile movies that lauded the benefits of
honking: "Gently tap the horn," spoke the tenor
of authority, "make others aware of your

Eldorado, Valiant,
Thunderbird, Riviera

presence." The honk our declamatory tool of
existence, still small voice of the boulevard. A
fellow hierophant punched my arm with
affection—I was one of the in-crowd, petitioning
at the altar of six cylinders, praying *give it up* to
the god of the pink slip or at least, his lackey
archangel,

Gabriel, Raphael,
Uriel, Michael

    and on the first day of year 16, I navigated
down 7 Mile Road, past Darby's burnt-out lot,
east on Livernois, past Chippewa Party Store
and the neon portal of Baker's Keyboard Lounge

Augustus B.   to Woodward's eight-lane testing ground that
sutured city to suburb, past all names I knew,
and the ball of my right foot felt the stirrings of
my exit from this city famous for strife, for its
mass-produced, affordable means of escape.

THE CARNIVAL

Faith Shearin

It will be spring when
the carnival comes to town.
Great tents will rise like bread
under the day's heat
and the ferris wheel will begin
its orbit. It is thrilling
how much can change
in a single night, how
an empty field can fill with color
and screams, with pale candy
spun from sugar and air.
Those cheap stuffed animals
were never meant to be won
and the fried dough
wasn't meant to be eaten.
If you walk through the fun house
there are mirrors that remember
who you were in a fairy tale:
a dwarf, a giant ruler
of beanstalks. As quickly
as it arrives it will vanish,
while you are humming
or sleeping, while you are lost
in thought. The grass in the field
will recall the shape of what
was pressed against it for a day,
or a week, then it will be as if
it never happened at all, as if
there are no fortune tellers,
no boxes of popcorn, no tickets
in your pocket, no buckets of rings
you toss into the dark.

PIONEER CARNIVAL #2
Patrick Young

FOLK RELIGIONS OF MICHIGAN

Marc Sheehan

for Jim Daniels

Witness the Cult of the Muscle Car
created in the heyday of the stamped metal
heaven which was Detroit. Still they roar
like Rintrah on long flat asphalt altars
sticky with the heat of brief summers.
The Church of the Place Up North
is preternaturally drafty and redolent
with the incense of mothballs and nostalgia,
while the Sacred Polish Wedding enables
the disrhythmic to dance like dervishes
and turns water into bourbon. The innermost
sanctums of that country are neon-lit and lined
by glassy-eyed mythical beasts. Winter
brings blizzards of biblical proportions
comprised of snowflakes identical to heathens.
The gospels all proclaim the same thing:
the Union Man is made in the image of God,
the Boat is holy for it floats on the Lake,
the Lake is holy for the mass baptisms it Affects,
the Baptized are holy in Form and in Flesh,
especially the Young among them.
The faithful ask guardian demons to deliver
them from one near-disaster to the next
with only a dented fender or broken
promise to atone for. Initiates know loneliness
is the only, but ubiquitous sin. Conjure
some weed, a box of Christ's blood
and a quorum of out-of-state friends returned
God knows why, and these hapless bastards
believe they're holy. Don't, under any
circumstances tell them otherwise.

JACOB STAP

Don Stap

1893 – 1976

Farmer and carpenter
soldier in the Old Country
stubborn old Dutchman alone for thirty years
in the whitewashed house falling in on itself
its walls leaning like a house of cards....

Each winter your dirt cellar was ankle-deep with walnuts.
The well water tasted like the night air in the woods
and there were bad dreams when your big face
swung like a lantern above me.
I closed my eyes tighter, but it was no good.

Now I fear your absence.
Forty-seven acres of your land is planted
with corn this year. Your land, I thought.
A new shopping center lights up a corner of the country sky.

It's all slipping away.
You never knew why,
and I see now that I won't either.
On your deathbed you were climbing a ladder.
My mother was trying to help you down.
Steady girlie, you said,
hold it for me at the bottom.

Train Trestle in the Woods
Michelle Calkins

CRITERIA

Phillip Sterling

You must be dead at least ten years.
You must have lived an unremarkable life
before that: a teacher, say, of unremarkable
students, a recluse, a furniture refurbisher,
or the humble liberator of unendangered species.

You must have welcomed children of your own
into the world and overall been a decent sort
of parent—surely made mistakes, but nothing
criminal. You must have done whatever you thought
would better your children's lives.

(And should one of them have hated you
for that: for giving them too much, or not
enough, or—even *after* the divorce—for introducing
to your bridal bed a lover much too young for you,
you'd likely have been forgiven…at the end…)

And if you'd failed at anything—at marriage,
employment, poetry—at least you'd tried,
you'd done your best. (Trying is all The Committee
will expect.) You must have loved your parents
for their love of you

and not for meek inheritance; you must have
cared for them when they required care, wiped
your father's foul behind, soaped his weary penis,
assured your mother *It will be okay…okay…*
And you must have known what it was like

to drive to the edge of the greatest lake
and climb the highest dune
and call out in your loudest, most joyous voice
the questions your soul had begged of you,
and not anticipate in return echo or reverberation

(as one would at Lover's Leap)
—however cold you may have been, however miserable
the wind, however old your vehicle, however long
you stood there
on the noble and ignorant sand.

LIFEBOAT

Alison Swan

Slipping down the Pitcher's thistle duneslope
at the edge of a freshwater sea
I recall the lifeboat, wooden on a wooden rack, paint peeling,

there, for so many years behind the foredunes,
miles from any road in the dune-grass shade of cottonwoods,
steps from the beach,

but nearly in the woods, so who'd have been there
to see, carry, launch, paddle, rescue, in this land scrap
without sidewalks,

land where what assembles, assembles according to some
fierce green fire,
even clouds tinged green, reflecting lake

and shore and out there: cold fresh water,
huge heavy body of it,
under condensation that's cloud, the sea in the sky.

We look up,
see doorways to space, stars, planets—Saturn, say,
which photographed in infrared looks elegant as the Titanic

pulling away from the White Star Dock for something
inimitable as outer space. Perhaps a child's thought,
perhaps others':

not enough lifeboats, absolutely sinkable. Surely
someone thinking: however clever, we're terrestrial
creatures who must stay warm or die.

Oh, to know the ones who took care here,
installed a boat on shifting land, where
creatures that crawl and fly are sole witnesses to the vigil,

to know the purchase of their steps, the stories they told,
the things they remembered,
what they lost, and how.

Turning

Lois Lovejoy

DIRECTIONS TO NORTH FISHTAIL BAY

Keith Taylor

If you paddle down past
the point where the eagles
hang out, you're almost there.
It's best like this--a hint
of fog flittering across
the lake before a breeze.
No sun, sky gray, but calm,
not a ripple or a wave.
Just round the next point, where
the sand drops away fast
under luminous deep green
water . . . And you made it!
Go now. It looks like rain.

You'll hear a hermit thrush
calling, hidden in the pines
or in a cedar swamp
where, when you look hard
into the dark, you will see
a profusion of iris,
almost purple and fresh
on this day, the very day you've
come alone to North Fishtail Bay.
There's thunder in the west.
Go now. It looks like rain.

HERRSHOFF

Lori Feldpausch

IN LANSING

Matthew Thorburn

Black coffee, for starters, and sun
sneaking through a scribble
of cloud. Holidays over and still
in from out east: you and me,
Kay, and cold day-old light—
dishwater or thereabouts. And pale,
the sky through these trees, blue
that's almost not blue; a bird's egg
or as if colors were verbs—

oranging, bluing—and you hadn't
said *blue*. Who loves January?
You see the steeple but the bell's
still broken, half-shined with ice.
And someone has to unplug
and take down these tangled strings
of lights, get the hose to spray
the salt off the Buick.
Three fingers of grass show up
through the snow. This is
hope? They're brown and yellow,
dying or dead. Couldn't

we cover all this more happily
in a kitcheny little still life? Freckled
bananas, fuzzy cheek of a peach,
the colander and the cheese
grater and the cheese?
Any waxy red wheel will do.
But already you've got
that look, like wherever you are
you wish you're someplace else—
though specific or
otherwise, you don't say. I say

I love how snow falls
on gray snow. And at night
you can see the stars here,
but really, how long do you want
to look at stars? If you say it
and say it and say it, even *happy*
sounds meaningless. Or *sad* or *sorry*
or *sublime*. My favorite word is *now*.
No, now my favorite word is
the one you're about to say.
"*Wish* is a funny word," you say,
pouring coffee. "You don't
hear it much anymore. Must be
we all got what we wanted."

MOONLIGHT SPILLS CRAZY UPON YOU, TEACHER OF THESE INMATES

Russell Thorburn

who glow with loss
and stroll around the store
with candy bars six months old.

You bless yourself in the name
of the sharpshooter
who can save your ass,

who follows you in his sights
and whose god is a bullet,
also in the name

of the razor-wire fences
stuttering over unredeemable acts
with knives, handguns, even axes.

This is no allegorical place you walk,
no man reading by a fire
or musing upon suffering

for the next issue of *Field*
magazine; the sharpshooter
can imbed a single bullet

deep into your brain
easily as knocking a can off a fence.
Under the Victorian edifice

this yard is a snowy place
of punishment five hundred miles
from their crimes in Detroit.

You in the dark light
bend your duck-beaked
boots toward class. Your voice

squeezed out to say hello.
And any comment from a hungry
inmate with chains

in his eye jerks
your own little chain
when he asks some

absurdity of you
and wants you to stand there
in fear,

your back to the moon
as big as this prison.
Nothing in here is not real.

DETROIT RIVER
Martha Ceccio

HOW TO GET THERE

Richard Tillinghast

Take the old road out of town.
Follow it
to where crabgrass snaggles up
through cracks in the concrete
and the day turns chilly.
The sky you thought
roofed summer and a lake,
picnics and the breast stroke and an Indigo
Bunting poised on the finial of a jack pine
contains, instead, Canada as seen on weather radar—
flurries, and an air-blast
from shores where ice-floes crumble off a glacier.

Bear south when you spot
a pillar of cumulus stacked up in the heartbreaking
dense blue above a bungalow where
a man and a woman in canvas lawn chairs
sit with their backs turned to each other,
and a tow-headed kid
maneuvers a nicked yellow toy dump truck
through a canyon ten inches deep,
while black ants observe.

Don't stop. You can't stop. Keep going
until you reach an intersection
where thunder percusses the shuddering inner spaces of sky
and lightens from within
cloud-pockets going dove-grey and gun-metal blue—
past a '48 straight-eight Buick
and thumb-sucking and daydreams,
past words like destination, and hot and cold,
and shame and regret
and starry diadem and Old Town canoe.

Keep driving
through the gap that opens between two novice heartbeats.
Before decades, before skies, before the first summer,
before any knowledge of roads and weather.
Back to where you are an infant again, open-mouthed,
and the whole world lies in wait for your wondering eyes.

Since You Always Threw Yourself out There, David Ruffin

Rodney Torreson

in that drizzle called life, such as onto the stage
for that impromptu audition with the Temptations,
maybe in the end it was easy for NBC
in the mini-series to throw the facts about.

Framed by your trademark black glasses,
while the other Temps danced a labyrinth behind you,
you would whirl around, throwing the microphone up
with one hand, snatching it with the other,

then hitting the floor with a leg split so crisp
that before you'd rise, the other Temps saw
the fortune of the moon and stars breaking your way,
your extended hand offering it to the crowd.

In the sun's turn-around time, you'd lunged
into stardom. Or maybe after the opening riff,
with its climbing guitar notes that scaled the heart,
you flung yourself into "My Girl"—

which Smokey Robinson wrote just for you—your baritone,
that gritty scuffle, going sweet as water over stones,
so that 700 miles away, in Terril, Iowa, cold wind
at our ribs, the song would strike up a blue sky:

"I've got sunshine on a cloudy day / and when it's cold outside, /
I've got the month of May," my brother Dean,
while the wind was reduced to a few breezy spumes, rigging
speakers in our upstairs window, so we could broadcast

"My Girl," all over the block—teaching it to the trees,
the flowers, even the crusty, world-weary sidewalks—
as if their cracks could take on your other trademark,
that break in your voice, so that even Beryl Coleman,

the old no non-sense justice of the peace, who lived next door,
would take store of your song, and her drapes would sway,
though back in Motown you were leaping into arrogance,
traveling solo in your mink-lined limo, while the rest of the band

hit the turnpike in a station wagon, you going so far
as to have your glasses painted on your limo,
as you hurled yourself into everything but rehearsals,
which you'd miss along with, later on, the concerts,

in your drug-induced exile, all of this leading to a hiss
in your skillet that broke the crying stillness,
and frost on the furniture, and you trying
to sign away your lady friend's Lincoln Continental

for $20 of cocaine, the Temptations soon voting you out
of the group. It was *then*, ironically, you'd show up
at gigs, flinging yourself onto the stage—for the shiny ache
you cosseted—while, for the Temptations

the stage lights stung, the audience weighing in with applause
when you'd pry the mike from the new front man's hands,
for "My Girl" or maybe "Ain't Too Proud to Beg"
or "Beauty's Only Skin Deep" or "I Wish It Would Rain."

And, my God, did it rain! The boiling truth of it is
you died in a Philadelphia crack house,
the limo driver then escorting you to a hospital.
Instead NBC tossed you out with the trash,

so that beneath the strain of streetlights, fans saw
your body being flung from a car into the ashen traffic,
as if it were only what you deserved,
and a funeral parlor pillow was what you were after.

MET

Katie Platte

TROUT OPENER

Rob VanderMolen

Sometimes nothing interesting happens—
The difference between youth and old age.
It was snowing in Cadillac, raining in Kalkaska

The way the stream muscled up so quickly
A remembered face, a remembered torso
But it's really shit when your health goes

Said Uncle Bunny—though he wasn't my uncle,
Someone else's, someone mired in a more
Tribal family, from what I gleaned from Bunny

He threw one can out the car window
Opened another. This beer is not so cold anymore.
But as I was saying, he tapped my shoulder

You hike out behind the house, see where bucks
Have been scraping their antlers, and here
We find stakes with orange streamers

For new township sewer lines—all
The round faces of ground animals looking
For leadership, paper trash from the highway

When I was a kid we'd reach under the bank
And pull steelhead out with our hands.
The next thing I knew I was wading in fronds

Batting bullets in New Guinea. All I tried
To think about were the more interesting parts
Of Alice—along with snow, deep shafts of winter…

A year later he died during an operation—
His flesh inside too rotten to be tied
Back together, or so said his son, a dapper jeweler

Thin smooth hands, beagle eyes

GRAVEL

Diane Wakoski

Yellow wings flash by the feeder,
    and make me realize I am not
alone. Standing at the glass door / watching,
    taking a risk, a glance
behind me—sense the shadow boy holding
    a piece of malachite.

It drips, a waterfall of green
    confusion. Yesterday there was
gravel under my foot
    on the kitchen floor and
for the first time I saw figures
    flying into the backyard,
black chevrons on their wings, which were like
    yellow sails.

Once I was a woman. Once I too was huge,
    perhaps a meteor. Now
having looked behind me,
    stunned by brightness and
immensity I rattle, a piece of
    gravel, infinite, infinitesimal,
to my Michigan kitchen floor. Never am I
    alone when I see those yellow vaulting

wings, always with the shadow boy who
    tracks in feathers and is surrounded by an
absinthe-green waterfall
        rushing into a pool,
        lit up with sunlight cast
           by the immense wings
           captioning and thudding at my door,
                a yellow furnace on the verge of swooping into
                the rain forest of old kitchens.

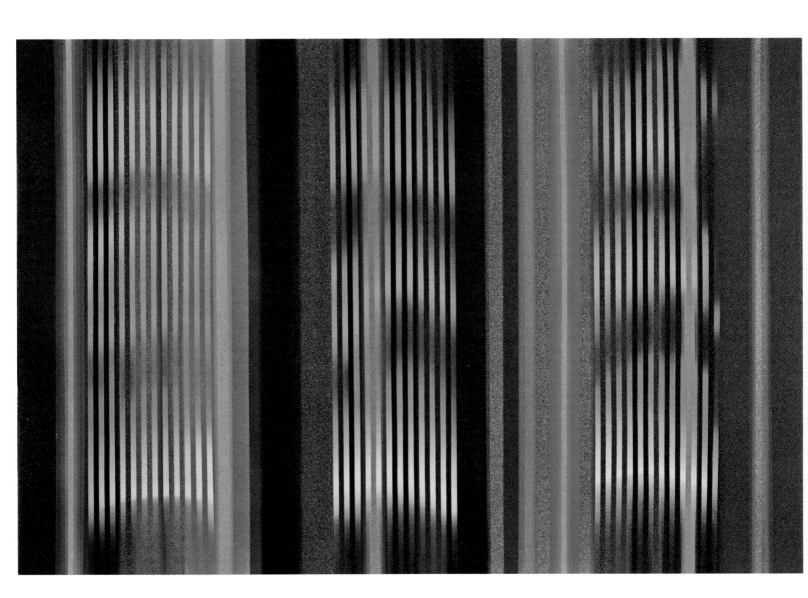

GREAT CRESTED FLYCATCHER'S SONG
Carol Hanna

WALK

Daneen Wardrop

At an intersection in Three Rivers, MI, he and I stand where a bridge arches over a garbled river on one side of us, an antique shop settles on the other. Is there a way we'd like to go? Quick, name the 10,000 things you love, do it before the *WALK* sign reappears. All the stops on Buddha's bamboo flute might be tuned to the same note so he need not choose intervals, and still he would play a suffusing melody, a tune with its own flexions, risings. The shop's window displays a dovecote for homing pigeons that once lodged on top of a department store. There was a clutching on all floors, coos for a roof. Though we feel our own flexions, as if there were desire in many thighs, the white-lit walker at the intersection light doesn't stroll yet. Perhaps we'll say something later about the loosed birds. We don't need to decide which way.

ALMOST SAVAGES

Angela Knauer Williams

The only blue I've seen for weeks is this body,
the color of my winter sky in plumage, a jay

fresh-killed for my assumption of doubt
for spring's awakening. And it will be

months until there is haven again for any of us.
Months until warmth is pliant in lake beds when

small fish will scatter away from my steps.
How many moonfish would the river hold

if you squeezed the banks together for an instant?
Each April I think of my father's smelt runs, inky

rimed artesian creek lined shoulder to shoulder three
men deep pressing in with nets and lanterns. Kerosene

hung in the piercing air. The rush of silver thicker than
a slot machine's payment. He'd bring his pails into

the kitchen before sunrise, line the table with yesterday's
paper, hand us each a shining knife, and pour the smelt

into a pile, some still alive, their flat eyes breathing.
It is not a field of poppies, this death. Nor is it the

shadow of a black willow, its head downcast unless
the wind builds coming in from the big lake. Steeling

against bleakness takes as much as hurtling upstream.
These willow leaves now, damp as nervous fingers

splayed across the fractured sidewalk are the jay's
feathers scattered from the cats' elation. The headless

corpse by the cellar door, their usual modus operandi.
First blood at the throat then sliced clean up the belly.

ALL THE ENDS
Jean Canavan

RESOLUTION: ICE STORM

John Woods

December 31, 1986

By late afternoon, the mist had thickened,
the maples sifting into dusk.
In the amiable shambles of people together,
we hungered around the lamps, the wine,
the pleasant chirp of dishware
on the last roll call of the year.
We vowed small disciplines on this night
of sackcloth and ashes.

All night the trees exploded,
power lines dragged and sparked.
Electricity closed its shops.

All across town, in the glare light
of the new year morning, trees bowed
in terrible metal, like Hiroshima,
a sunken ship, the wreckage of Eden.
Townsmen toured the ice museum
in the crystal discipline of cameras:
the cold spectacles, the oxides of silver.

Grandpa told us we have promises to keep,
so the sun opened its busy stores.
The rose bowl of the TV stuttered on.
Half our sugar maple, trebled in gravity, lay
in the stiff, gray grass of the front lawn.
I could see through the ice to its rude mottle.
It is difficult to look out
from such beauty.

CITYLIGHTS 81
Stephen Magsig

Acknowledgements

Tom Andrews: "At Burt Lake" from *Random Symmetries*. Copyright © 2003 by Tom Andrews. Reprinted with the permission of The Permissions Company, Inc., on behalf of Oberlin College Press. *www.oberlin.edu/ocpress*

James Armstrong: "Say Yes to Michigan" appears here for the first time in print.

Cullen Bailey Burns: "Change" from *Slip* (New Issues Poetry & Prose).
Copyright © 2013 by Cullen Bailey Burns.

Jackie Bartley: "Freighters Return to the Harbor" appears here for the first time in print.

Elinor Benedict: "The Burn" from *The Tree Between Us* (March Street Press), and *Late News from the Wilderness* (Main Street Rag). Copyrights © 1997 and © 2009 by Elinor Benedict.

Terry Blackhawk: "Down in Detroit" appears here for the first time in print.

Gladys Cardiff: "Setting up the Fountain in Rochester Municipal Park: Late May" appears here for the first time in print.

Susanna Childress: "Mother as Opalescent Bottle" from *Entering the House of Awe* (New Issues Poetry & Prose). Copyright © 2011 by Susanna Childress.

Patricia Clark: "Missing" from *My Father on a Bicycle*. Copyright © 2005 by Patricia Clark. Reprinted with the permission of Michigan State University Press.

David Cope: "The dharma at last" from *Turn the Wheel* (Vox Humana Press). Copyright © 2003 by David Cope. Reprinted with the permission of the author.

Jim Daniels: "Aerial View of Warren, Michigan" from *Having a Little Talk with Capital P Poetry*. Copyright © 2011 by Jim Daniels. Reprinted with the permission of The Permissions Company, Inc., on behalf of Carnegie Mellon University Press. *www.cmu.edu/universitypress*

Michael Delp: "Letter to Jim Harrison" appears here for the first time in print.

Toi Derricotte: "The Weakness" from *Captivity*. Copyright © 1989 by Toi Derricotte. Reprinted with the permission of University of Pittsburgh Press.

Chris Dombrowski: "Naïve Melody" from *Earth Again*. Copyright © 2013 Wayne State University Press. Reprinted with the permission of Wayne State University Press.

Jack Driscoll: "Houdini" from *Building the Cold from Memory* (Greenfield Review Press). Copyright © 1989 by Jack Driscoll. Reprinted with the permission of the author.

Stuart Dybek: "Milk Train" originally appeared in *Smartish Place* and *Poetry Daily*.

Nancy Eimers: "Shipwreck Museum, Whitefish Point" appears here for the first time in print.

Robert Fanning: "What Is Written on the Leaves" appears here for the first time in print.

Lisa Fishman: "[Questions about snakes]" from *Current*. Copyright © 2011 by Lisa Fishman, by permission of Parlor Press. "Instructions/ Confessions" and "[from 'Creature']" from *The Happiness Experiment*. Copyright © 2007 by Lisa Fishman. Reprinted with the permission of The Permissions Company, Inc., on behalf of Ahsahta Press. *www.ahsahtapress.boisestate.edu*

Artists

Mary Brodbeck, originally trained in industrial design, worked in the West Michigan furniture industry for a dozen years before shifting to image making in the 1990's. Brodbeck's award winning Great Lakes woodblock prints are in art collections around the world including her *Sleeping Bear Dunes* series at the Detroit Institute of Arts. She is currently working on a film about the Japanese woodblock printmaking process.
www.marybrodbeck.com

Michelle Calkins studied art at Hope College in Holland, Michigan. "In my work I emphasize quality, integrity and spontaneity. Since childhood I have found solace in the creation of art. It is my gift and I try not to waste it. My media of choice are oil painting, sculpture and photography. For me, the three disciplines borrow from each other making each one stronger!"

Jean Canavan's watercolor still life and landscapes often reflect her interest in the transitions of light and shadow, and strive to express a sense of memory of time and place. She is a long-time resident of Saline and teaches Watercolor and Travel Journaling when she is not creating and exhibiting her own works.
www.jeanmcanavan.com

Nathan Caplan is an emeritus professor in psychology and emeritus research scientist at the University of Michigan. Never a professional photographer, he has been a recent winner in Individual and Portfolio competitions sponsored by *Black and White*, the premier international fine art photography magazine.

Martha Ceccio received a BS in Fine Arts from Amherst College, and a BFA from Boston University, and an MFA from the University of Michigan. Her work, including photography and encaustic, as well as traditional oil paintings, are shown in several galleries, in Michigan and nationally.
www.marthaceccio.com

Karin Wagner Coron is an Ann Arbor native currently living in Ypsilanti, Michigan with her husband Steve. She is a graduate of Eastern Michigan University with a BFA in Painting and Drawing. She has owned and operated Format Framing and Gallery since 1986, and is currently a member of the WSG Gallery in Ann Arbor.

Steve Coron was born in northern Michigan and began teaching art at the age of sixteen. Coron is the head of the Visual Arts Department at Community High School in Ann Arbor, where he teaches courses in photography, digital imaging, drawing and painting, multi-media, and Italian Art and Culture.

Lori Feldpausch: My love for the outdoors and interest in art has been life-long. I have a keen sense of simple places and spaces that translate well to my artwork. I feel a sense of history when I paint, a consecutiveness to the source of information, more than just a concept, they are capturing a feeling from the heart, an unwritten word. A soul connection, from the painter to the viewer.

Steve Gilzow has done seventeen covers for the *Ann Arbor Observer*, and has won an award in the Michigan Water Color Society's annual competition. He has served as an artist-in-residence at Porcupine Mountains Wilderness State Park, and was also one of sixteen artists invited to contribute to the 2012 *Stand in the Place Where You Live* exhibit curated by the Legacy Land Conservancy and the Chelsea Center for the Arts.

David Grath's early career focused on figurative painting and bronze casting, but he is best recognized for his Michigan landscapes. He has been painting for sixty years, and has shown in Chicago, Detroit, and Cincinnati, as well as Leelanau County and Traverse City, Michigan. He maintains a gallery in Northport, Michigan.

Ladislav R. Hanka lives in Kalamazoo, Michigan and exhibits internationally. His work examines themes of life, death and transfiguration – nature as the crucible in which man finds a reflection of his own life and meaning. He's had about 100 one-man shows and his etchings can be found in about 100 public collections worldwide. The Permanent Archive of his works is housed at Special Collections: Western Michigan University.
www.ladislavhanka.com

Carol Hanna mixes science and art, using visual language to represent the color of birds and the notes of their songs. She has lived in the Ann Arbor area most of her adult life and exhibited both in Michigan and nationally. Her works are in private, corporate, and university collections. She received both a BFA and an MA degree from Eastern Michigan University.
www.carolhanna.com

Lois Lovejoy lives in Ann Arbor and uses watercolor or pastel to portray the color, texture and spirit of landscape. Her painting evolved from her career as a graphic artist and book illustrator. Her work, some of which is in private collections, can be viewed in Michigan juried exhibitions and the annual June Chelsea Painters Fair.

Stephen Magsig's Detroit paintings capture scenes of daily life and reflect a distinctly American landscape where industry, urban and nature collide. They are a visual record of the quiet beauty in the everyday scene. Places that exist in silence, unrevered and waiting to be discovered. Scenes of vanishing industry, urban ruins, sunlit houses, storefronts and the urban prairie.

Alanna Pfeffer studied journalism at the University of Maine and is currently Marketing Assistant at SEE Eyewear in Southfield, MI. She is a freelance photographer and graphic designer. In her photography, she focuses on portraying Detroit in a positive light.
www.alannapfeffer.com

Katie Platte is an artist who works in intaglio, woodcut and letterpress. She is the studio coordinator and an instructor at the Kalamazoo Book Arts Center, a nonprofit where artists and book enthusiasts of all kinds gather to collaborate and celebrate books and the many arts that inform them: paper making, printmaking, letterpress, creative writing, and bookbinding.

Meridith Ridl is an artist and an art teacher with a BA from the College of Wooster and MFA from the University of Michigan. She is represented by Lafontsee Galleries in Grand Rapids, MI and has exhibited her work at the Grand Rapids Art Museum, the University of Toledo, the Butler Museum of American Art, and the Museum of Contemporary Art in Queretaro, Mexico.

Erin Scott holds an MFA from CSU-Fullerton and has been a college art educator since the early 1990s. Employing subject matter that ranges from still life to figures, her paintings reveal intimate and sometimes shocking narratives with a recurring theme of inner strength and triumph. Erin currently lives in Detroit.

Craig Seaver received a BS in Chemistry from Western Michigan University before beginning his photography career from his home in Traverse City. Seaver finds inspiration from his forays into the heart of northern Michigan. He uses his camera to express his inner voice and strives to push the creative boundaries of photography. Seaver's work is displayed in fine galleries throughout northern Michigan and on his website:
www.traversecityfaces.com

Tom Walsh grew up in Boston. He attended Massachusetts College of Art, majoring in painting and printmaking. He is retired and lives in Ann Arbor. With the exception of Red Sox games, he's busy working on his art. *www.morecontrast.net*

Mary Whalen is a photographer and arts educator living in Kalamazoo, Michigan. She has been a professional photographer for 25 years. She has been a Lincoln Center Institute teaching artist in the Kalamazoo area since 2002. She regularly exhibits work in the Southwest Michigan area and has been involved with the SOHO20 Chelsea Gallery in NYC since 2001.

Nancy Wolfe teaches a summer workshop called 'The Visual Journal,' at Northwestern Michigan College in Traverse City, Michigan, a biannual workshop for Wayne State University's Art Therapy Department, and she is an Adjunct Professor at Eastern Michigan University. "I've always wanted to be a poet and my paintings, for me, are as close as I come to poetry. My artwork is a visual connection to my love for the turns and tricks of language." *www.nancywolfe.com*

Patrick Young retired from the University of Michigan in 2012 after forty years, where he served as a webmaster, a Director of Exhibitions and Communications, and as a Faculty Advisor on digital imaging and printing. He now works as a freelance photographer/digital imaging specialist and is sole proprietor of Michigan Imaging, specializing in photography of fine art and large format printing.

Poets

Tom Andrews (1961–2001) graduated from Hope College and earned his MFA at the University of Virginia. Andrews published three books of poems, a memoir, *Codeine Diary*, about his coming to terms with his hemophilia, and edited two collections of essays in his lifetime. Oberlin College Press published *Random Symmetries: The Collected Poems of Tom Andrews*, a posthumous volume, in 2002.

James Armstrong grew up in Kalamazoo, where he learned to love the rolling hills and overgrown farm fields of southwestern Michigan. He is the author of two books, *Monument in a Summer Hat* (New Issues Press, 1999) and *Blue Lash* (Milkweed Editions, 2006). Armstrong is currently a Professor of English at Winona State University in Winona, Minnesota.

Cullen Bailey Burns grew up in Kalamazoo, Michigan and now lives in Minneapolis, MN. The author of *Slip* and *Paper Boat*, her poems have appeared in *The Denver Quarterly*, *Rattle*, *Hayden's Ferry Review*, among many others. She is a teacher and beekeeper and spends her summers at her small farm in northern Minnesota.

Jackie Bartley sews and gardens in Holland, Michigan. Her poems and essays have appeared in many journals including *Under the Sun*, *Southampton Review*, and *Poet Lore*. She aspires to Rilke's image, "If the drink is bitter, turn yourself to wine."

Elinor Benedict has published five chapbooks of poetry and won the May Swenson Award for her first full poetry collection, *All That Divides Us*. Her second collection, *Late News from the Wilderness*, deals with the wilderness of the Upper Peninsula of Michigan. Although she grew up in Tennessee, she has called Rapid River, Michigan, her home for forty years.

Terry Blackhawk is the founder and director of Detroit's acclaimed InsideOut Literary Arts Project, a poets-in-schools program serving over 5,000 youth per year. Terry's poetry collections include *Body & Field*, *Escape Artist* (selected by Molly Peacock for the John Ciardi Prize), *The Light Between*, and two chapbooks, *Trio: Voices from the Myths* and *Greatest Hits 1989-2003*.

Gladys Cardiff is an enrolled member of the Eastern Band of Cherokee. Her books include *A Bare Unpainted Table*, and *To Frighten a Storm*. Cardiff has recently retired from Oakland University and moved to Seattle where she is working on a manuscript of poems and a family history of the Owl family, her father's lineage.

Susanna Childress has published two books of poetry: *Jagged with Love* (winner of the 2005 Brittingham Prize), and *Entering the House of Awe* (winner of the 2012 Society of Midland Authors Award). She is a member of the band Ordinary Neighbors, whose full-length album *The Necessary Dark* borrows from her writing. She lives in Holland, MI.

Patricia Clark is Poet-in-Residence and Professor in the Department of Writing at Grand Valley State University. Author of four volumes of poetry, Patricia's latest book is *Sunday Rising*. She is also the author of a chapbook, *Given the Trees*, in the Voices from the American Land series.

David Cope is the Poet Laureate of Grand Rapids. He is the author of seven books and editor of *Song of the Owashtanong: Grand Rapids Poetry in the 21st Century*. He has won a Pushcart Prize, and an award in Literature from the American Academy of Arts and Letters. He is the editor and publisher of *Big Scream* / Nada Press. Archive: David Cope Papers at University of Michigan Special Collections Library.

Jim Daniels' most recent book of poems, *Birth Marks*, was published by BOA Editions in 2013. His latest collection of short fiction, *Trigger Man: More Tales of the Motor City*, was published in 2011 by Michigan State University Press. A native of Detroit, Daniels teaches at Carnegie Mellon University in Pittsburgh, where he is the Thomas Stockham Baker Professor of English.

Michael Delp is co-editor of the "Made in Michigan" book series. His most recent book, *As If We Were Prey*, is a collection of short stories from Wayne State University Press.

Toi Derricotte is the author of five books of poetry, and a literary memoir, *The Black Notebooks*, which won the 1998 Anisfield-Wolf Book Award for Non-Fiction and was a New York Times Notable Book of the Year. Her honors include the 2012 Paterson Poetry Prize for Sustained Literary Achievement and the 2012 PEN/Voelcker Award for Poetry. With Cornelius Eady, she co-founded Cave Canem Foundation, North America's premiere "home for black poetry."

Chris Dombrowski is the author of *By Cold Water*, and *Earth Again*, both published by Wayne State University Press. He was born in Lansing, Michigan.

Jack Driscoll is the author of four novels, four poetry collections, and the AWP Short Fiction Award winner *Wanting Only to Be Heard*. He has received the Barnes & Noble Discover Great New Writers Award, the PEN/Nelson Algren Fiction Award, the Pushcart Editors' Book Award, Pushcart Prizes, PEN Syndicated Fiction Awards, and *Best American Short Stories* citations. He currently teaches in Pacific University's acclaimed low-residency MFA.

Stuart Dybek is Professor Emeritus at Western Michigan University and a member of the permanent faculty in WMU's Prague Summer Program. His books of poetry are *Streets in Their Own Ink* (FSG) and *Brass Knuckles* (Carnegie Mellon Press). Dybek is also the author of several books of fiction.

Nancy Eimers is the author of four poetry collections: *Oz*, *A Grammar to Waking*, *No Moon* and *Destroying Angel*. She has been the recipient of a Nation "Discovery" Award, a Whiting Writers Award, two NEA Fellowships, and a Pushcart Prize; she teaches Creative Writing at Western Michigan University.

Robert Fanning is the author of *American Prophet*, *The Seed Thieves*, and *Old Bright Wheel*. A graduate of the University of Michigan and Sarah Lawrence College, he is an Associate Professor of Creative Writing at Central Michigan University. He is also the founder and facilitator of the Wellspring Literary Series in Mt. Pleasant, MI.
www.robertfanning.wordpress.com

Lisa Fishman's most recent books are *F L O W E R   C A R T* and *Current*. She is also the author of *The Happiness Experiment*; *Dear, Read*; and *The Deep Heart's Core Is a Suitcase*. An Associate Professor of English at Columbia College Chicago, Fishman is a native of Michigan (Leelanau County and metro-Detroit). She lives on a farm in Orfordville, Wisconsin.

Linda Nemec Foster is the author of nine collections of poetry including *Amber Necklace from Gdansk* and *Talking Diamonds*. Foster's work has been honored with awards from ArtWorks Michigan, the National Writer's Voice, and the Academy of American Poets. She founded the Contemporary Writers Series at Aquinas College. *www.lindanemecfoster.com*

Matthew Gavin Frank is the author of the nonfiction books, *Preparing the Ghost: An Essay Concerning the Giant Squid and the Man Who First Photographed It*, *Pot Farm*, and *Barolo*, the poetry books, *The Morrow Plots*, *Warranty in Zulu*, and *Sagittarius Agitprop*, and the chapbooks, *Four Hours to Mpumalanga* and *Aardvark*. He teaches creative writing in the MFA Program at Northern Michigan University, where he is the Nonfiction Editor of *Passages North*.

Joy Gaines-Friedler is the author of *Like Vapor* and *Dutiful Heart*. She has won several awards including First Place for a series of poems based on the journal of her friend Jim who died from AIDS. Joy teaches Advanced Poetry and Creative Writing for non-profits in the Detroit area, including workshops with homeless young adults and families of victims of homicide.

Dan Gerber's eighth collection of poems, *Sailing through Cassiopeia* (Copper Canyon Press 2012) received the 2013 Society of Midland Authors Award for Poetry. Also the author of three novels, a book of short stories, and two nonfiction books, his work has appeared in *Poetry*, *Narrative*, *The New Yorker*, *Massachusetts Review*, and *Best American Poetry*.

Mary Jo Firth Gillett's poetry collection, *Soluble Fish*, won the Crab Orchard Series First Book Award. She's also published four award-winning chapbooks, most recently *Dance Like a Flame*. She won the N.Y. Open Voice Poetry Award and a 2012 Kresge Artist Fellowship in the Literary Arts. Her MFA is from Vermont College.

Linda Gregerson's fifth collection of poetry, *The Selvage*, was published by Houghton Mifflin Harcourt in 2012. Her third book, *Waterborne*, won the 2003 Kingsley Tufts Poetry Award; *Magnetic North* was a finalist for the 2007 National Book Award. Gregerson is the Caroline Walker Bynum Distinguished University Professor of English at the University of Michigan.

Mariela Griffor is the director of Marick Press. Her books include *House* (Mayapple Press) and *The Psychiatrist* (Eyewear Publishing). Her translation of *Canto General* by Pablo Neruda is forthcoming from Tupelo Press.

Robert Haight has published three poetry collections, *Water Music*, *Emergences and Spinner Falls* and *Feeding Wild Birds*, and written essays and articles on fly fishing, the environment, education and spirituality for a variety of anthologies, journals and magazines. He teaches writing, literature and meditation at Kalamazoo Valley Community College and lives in Cass County.

francine j. harris' first collection, *allegiance*, reached the number one spot on the national poetry bestseller's list and was a finalist for the 2013 Kate Tufts Discovery Award and *ForeWord Reviews* Book of the Year. Originally from Detroit, she is a Cave Canem fellow and is the Front Street Writers Writer-in-Residence in Traverse City, Michigan for the 2013/14 school year.

Jim Harrison is the author of thirty books, including *Legends of the Fall* and *Dalva*. His work has been translated into 24 languages and produced as four feature-length films. As a young poet he co-edited *Sumac* (with Dan Gerber) and earned a National Endowment for the Arts grant and a Guggenheim Fellowship. In 2007, he was elected into the Academy of American Arts & Letters.

Bob Hicok's latest book is *Elegy Owed* (Copper Canyon Press, 2013).

Conrad Hilberry was a professor of English at Kalamazoo College in Michigan from 1962 to 1998. He is the author of *Encounter on Burrows Hill and Other Poems*, *Rust*, *Man in the Attic*, *Knowing Rivers*, *You Know the Shape and Bias*, *The Moon Seen as a Slice of Pineapple*, *Jacob's Dancing Tune*, *Sorting the Smoke: New and Selected Poems*, *Player Piano*, and *The Fingernail of Luck*.

Dennis Hinrichsen is the author of six books of poetry. His most recent are *Rip-tooth* (2010 Tampa Poetry Prize) and *Kurosawa's Dog* (2008 FIELD Poetry Prize). An earlier work, *Detail from* The Garden of Earthly Delights, won the 1999 Akron Poetry Prize. He currently resides in Lansing.

Amorak Huey, a former newspaper editor, teaches writing at Grand Valley State University. He holds an MFA from Western Michigan University, and his poems have appeared in *The Best American Poetry 2012*, *Hayden's Ferry Review*, *The Cincinnati Review*, *Rattle*, *Caketrain*, and other journals.

Austin Hummell teaches Mythology, Film and Poetry Writing, and is an Associate Professor of English. His books are *Poppy*, winner of the 2003 Del Sol Press Poetry Prize, and *The Fugitive Kind*, winner of the University of Georgia Press's Contemporary Poetry Series.

Lizzie Hutton's first book of poems is *She'd Waited Millennia*. Hutton has received the Wabash Prize, a Meader Award and a Hopwood Award; her essays and poems have appeared in the *Yale Review*, *New England Review* and *Antioch Review*, among other journals. She is currently pursuing her PhD at the University of Michigan.

David James' second book, *She Dances Like Mussolini*, won the 2010 Next Generation Indie book award. He has also published four chapbooks, and more than thirty of his one-act plays have been produced from New York to California. He teaches writing at Oakland Community College.

D.R. James's first book is *Since Everything Is All I've Got*, and his three chapbooks are *A Little Instability without Birds*, *Lost Enough*, and *Psychological Clock*. He lives in Holland, where he has been teaching writing and literature at Hope College for 28 years.

Rhoda Janzen is the author of a poetry collection, *Babel's Stair*, and the NY Times #1 bestseller, *Mennonite in a Little Black Dress*, a finalist for both the 2010 James Thurber Humor Award and the Lily Fellows Arlin G. Meyer Prize for Imaginative Writing. Her memoir, *Does This Church Make Me Look Fat?*, was a finalist for the 2013 Books for a Better Life Award. *www.rhodajanzen.com*

Jonathan Johnson is the author of two books of poems, *Mastodon, 80% Complete* and *In the Land We Imagined Ourselves*, the nonfiction book *Hannah and the Mountain: Notes Toward a Wilderness Fatherhood*, and the play *Ode* about John Keats and Fanny Brawne. Johnson teaches in the MFA program at Eastern Washington University.

Laura Kasischke was born in Grand Rapids, Michigan and teaches in the MFA program at the University of Michigan. Her books of poetry include *Wild Brides* (1992), *Fire and Flower* (1998), *Dance and Disappear* (2002), *Gardening in the Dark* (2004), *Lilies Without* (2007), and *Space, in Chains* (2011), which won the National Book Critics Circle Award.

Josie Kearns was born and raised in Flint. She is the author of *New Numbers* and *The Theory of Everything*, as well as two chapbooks and a non-fiction book about laid off autoworkers in new careers: *Life After the Line*. The former director of the Young Writers Academy and the Visiting Writers Series in Flint, she teaches writing and literature full-time at the University of Michigan.

Elizabeth Kerlikowske is a Michigan native. She is a poet, visual artist, and mother of three. Her publications include dozens of print and online journals, five books of poetry, and inclusion in several anthologies. She would never live anywhere else.

Judith Kerman is a poet, performer and artist with broad cultural and scholarly interests. She has published eight books or chapbooks of poetry, most recently *Galvanic Response* from March Street Press.

L.S. Klatt is currently an associate professor of literature and creative writing at Calvin College. "Ford" comes from a series of prose poems that take the names of American corporations as their titles. Klatt's first book, *Interloper*, was awarded the Juniper Prize for Poetry. His second collection, *Cloud of Ink*, won the Iowa Poetry Prize.

Kimberly Kolbe's work has won awards from The Michigan Poet and Western Michigan University, and has appeared at *AGNI on-line*, and in *Passages North* and *Hayden's Ferry Review*. She is from Walkerville, Michigan.

David Dodd Lee is the author of *The Coldest Winter On Earth, Poems 1998-2011*; *Orphan, Indiana*; *The Nervous Filaments*; *Sky Booths in the Breath Somewhere*, *The Ashbery Erasure Poems*; *Abrupt Rural*; and *Downsides of Fish Culture*. His eighth book, *Animalities*, is forthcoming from Four Way Books. Lee is an Assistant Professor of English at Indiana University South Bend.

Philip Levine was the eighteenth United States Poet Laureate for 2011-2012. As well as having received two National Book Awards, Levine is also the recipient of the National Book Critics Award and the Ruth Lily prize. He divides his time between Brooklyn, NY, and Fresno, CA.

M.L. Liebler is the author of 13 books, and he is St. Clair Shores' first Poet Laureate. He has taught English and Labor Studies at Wayne State University since 1980, and is the founding director of The National Writer's Voice Project in Detroit and the Springfed Arts: Metro Detroit Writers. Liebler received the Barnes & Noble/*Poets & Writers* "Writers for Writers" Award, and his anthology, *Working Words: Punching the Clock and Kicking Out the Jams*, won the Michigan Notable Book Award for 2011. *www.mlliebler.com*

Thomas Lynch is the author of five collections of poems, a book of short fictions, and three collections of essays including *The Undertaking*, which won The American Book Award, The Heartland Prize and was a finalist for the National Book Award. He has taught at Wayne State University's Mortuary School, University of Michigan's Graduate Program in Creative Writing and the Candler School of Theology at Emory University. Since 1974 he has been the funeral director in Milford, Michigan.

Naomi Long Madgett has been well recognized for her contributions as poet, publisher/editor, educator, and has most recently received the 2012 Kresge Eminent Artist Award. She is author of ten books of poems, the first published when she was only seventeen years old. Her early out-of-print books are now available under the title, *Remembrances of Spring: Collected Early Poems*.

Corey Marks is the author *The Radio Tree*, winner of the Green Rose Prize, and *Renunciation*, a National Poetry Series selection. He grew up in Michigan and still spends his summers in Grand Marais. He teaches at University of North Texas.

Peter Markus is the author of a novel, *Bob, or Man on Boat*, as well as the collections of fiction *Good, Brother*, *The Singing Fish*, and *We Make Mud*. He was named a Kresge Arts in Detroit fellow in Literary Arts in 2012 and teaches as a poet-in-the-schools with the InsideOut Literary Arts Project of Detroit.

Dave Marlatt holds a MFA in Creative Writing from Western Michigan University. His poems have appeared in *Poetry Northwest*, *Nimrod*, *Passages North*, *The Sycamore Review*, *The Icarus Review*, *The Big Two-Hearted*, and other journals. He is the author of *A Hog Slaughtering Woman: Poems*, and he plays Irish fiddle with the band Whiskey Before Breakfast.

Gail Martin is the author of *The Hourglass Heart* and *Begin Empty-Handed*, winner of the Perugia Press Poetry Prize. Recent work appears in *Alaska Quarterly Review*, *Tar River Review* and *Poet Lore*. Martin works as a psychotherapist in private practice in Kalamazoo, MI.

Kathleen McGookey is the author of *Whatever Shines*, *October Again*, and a book of translations of French writer Georges Godeau's prose poems, *We'll See*. Her chapbook *Mended* is forthcoming from Kattywompus Press. She lives with her family in Middleville, Michigan.

Judith Minty is Professor Emeritus of English and Women's Studies at Humbolt State University and lives in New Era, Michigan. She is the author of *Lake Songs and Other Fears* (1973), *Dancing the Fault: Poems by Judith Minty* (1991), and *Walking with the Bear* (2000).

Ander Monson is the author of a number of paraphernalia including a website, a decoder wheel, several chapbooks, as well as six books including the forthcoming book-in-a-box *Letter to a Future Lover* (Graywolf Press, 2015). Originally from Houghton, he now lives in Tucson, Arizona.

Julie Moulds grew up in North Muskegon, and earned her B.A. at Hope College. She taught Children's Literature at several colleges and taught Creative Writing to children. After a sixteen-year battle with non-Hodgkin's lymphoma, Julie passed away in 2008.

Amy Newday's poems have appeared in *Poetry East*, *Rhino*, *Notre Dame Review*, *Calyx*, and *Flyway: Journal of Writing and Environment*. She directs the Writing Center at Kalamazoo College and co-owns Harvest of Joy Farm LLC, a community-supported vegetable farm in Shelbyville.

William Olsen is the author of five collections of poetry, including *Sand Theory*. He has received fellowships from the Guggenheim Foundation and the National Endowment for the Arts. He teaches at Western Michigan University and lives in Kalamazoo.

Anne-Marie Oomen is author of *Pulling Down the Barn* and *House of Fields*, both Michigan Notable Books, *An American Map: Essays*; a collection of poetry, *Uncoded Woman*; and seven plays, including *Secrets of Luuce Talk Tavern*, winner of the 2012 CTAM contest. She is instructor of creative writing at Interlochen Arts Academy, ICCA Writer's Retreat, and Solstice MFA at Pine Manor College, MA.

Miriam Pederson lives in Grand Rapids where she is a Professor Emeritus of English at Aquinas College. She earned an MFA degree in Creative Writing from Western Michigan University. She is the author of the chapbook, *This Brief Light*. Pederson's poems in collaboration with sculpture created by her husband, Ron Pederson, are exhibited in area and regional galleries.

Susan Blackwell Ramsey got her BA from Kalamazoo College and, forty years later, her MFA from The University of Notre Dame. She was included in *Best American Poetry 2009* and her book *A Mind Like This* won the Prairie Schooner Poetry Book Prize from University of Nebraska Press. She teaches at the Kalamazoo Institute of Arts and lives in Kalamazoo.

Greg Rappleye lives near Grand Haven. He is the author of several chapbooks and books of poetry, including *A Path Between Houses*, which won the Brittingham Prize, and *Figured Dark*, which was runner-up for the Dorset Prize. He is Corporation Counsel for Ottawa County and teaches in the English Department at Hope College.

Josh Rathkamp was born in Saginaw, Michigan. His first collection of poetry, *Some Nights No Cars At All*, is distributed by Copper Canyon. His work has appeared in numerous literary journals and public art projects, including *APR*, *Arts and Letters*, *Poet Lore*, *Rattle*, and *Gulf Coast*. He is the Director of the Creative Writing Program at Mesa Community College.

Christine Rhein is the author of *Wild Flight*, winner of the Walt McDonald Prize. Her poems have appeared in *The Gettysburg Review*, *The Southern Review*, and *Michigan Quarterly Review*, and have been selected for *Poetry Daily*, *Verse Daily*, *The Writer's Almanac*, and *Best New Poets 2007*. A former auto engineer, she lives in Brighton. *www.christinerhein.com*

Jack Ridl's collections are *Broken Symmetry*, recipient of the 2006 Society of Midland Authors Award, *Losing Season*, and *Practicing to Walk Like a Heron*. His chapbook, *Against Elegies*, was selected by then Poet Laureate Billy Collins for the Center for Book Arts (NYC) Award. Jack taught for 38 years and was named Michigan Professor of the Year by the Carnegie Foundation. More than 75 of his students are now published authors. *www.ridl.com*

Ron Riekki's books include *U.P.* and *The Way North: Collected Upper Peninsula New Works*, which features writing by Ellen Airgood, Janeen Rastall, Andrea Scarpino, and 40 other talented Yooper-connected authors. Riekki has a PhD in Literature & Creative Writing from Western Michigan University.

John Rybicki was born and raised in Detroit. He is the author of *Traveling at High Speeds*, *We Bed Down Into Water*, and *When All the World Is Old*. Rybicki has been a writer-in-residence at Alma College, and currently teaches poetry to young writers through the InsideOut Literary Arts Project and Wings of Hope Hospice.

Mary Ann Samyn is the author of five collections of poetry—most recently, *Beauty Breaks In* and *My Life in Heaven*, winner of the 2012 *FIELD* Prize. She's a Professor of English at West Virginia University where she directs the MFA program.

Teresa Scollon is a native of Michigan's thumb and alumna and former writer-in-residence at Interlochen Arts Academy. Recipient of a National Endowment for the Arts fellowship, she is the author of *To Embroider the Ground with Prayer*, and the chapbook *Friday Nights the Whole Town Goes to the Basketball Game*. She lives in Traverse City, Michigan. *www.teresascollon.com*

Herbert S. Scott (1931-2006) is the author of *Sleeping Woman, Disguises, Groceries, Durations,* and *The Other Life: Selected Poems.* He taught at Western Michigan University where he was the Gwen Frostic Professor of Creative Writing and founded New Issues Poetry & Prose.

Heather Sellers is a professor of English at the University of South Florida where she teaches creative nonfiction and poetry. She is the author of the children's book *Spike and Cubby's Ice Cream Island Adventure,* three volumes of poetry, three books on the craft of writing, the short story collection, *Georgia Under Water,* a Barnes & Noble Discover Great New Writers selection, and a memoir, *You Don't Look Like Anyone I Know.*

Diane Seuss is the author of *Four-Legged Girl* (forthcoming from Graywolf Press, 2015); *Wolf Lake, White Gown Blown Open* (winner of the Juniper Prize for Poetry); and *It Blows You Hollow.* Diane has received a Pushcart Prize, and was the MacLean Distinguished Visiting Writer at Colorado College. She is Writer in Residence at Kalamazoo College.

Patty Seyburn has published three books of poems: *Hilarity, Mechanical Cluster,* and *Diasporadic.* Her fourth collection, *Perfecta,* is forthcoming from What Books Press. She is an Associate Professor at California State University, Long Beach and co-editor of *POOL: A Journal of Poetry.*
www.poolpoetry.com

Faith Shearin is the author of three books of poetry: *The Owl Question* (winner of the May Swenson Award), *The Empty House,* and *Moving the Piano.* Recent work has appeared in *Alaska Quarterly Review, The Southern Review* and on *The Writer's Almanac.* Her work also appears in *The Autumn House Anthology of Contemporary Poets* and in *Good Poems, American Places.*

Marc J. Sheehan is the author of two poetry collections: *Greatest Hits* and *Vengeful Hymns,* which won the Richard Snyder Award. He has published interviews with a number of prominent writers including Richard Ford, Jim Harrison, Michael Moore and Jane Smiley. He is Communications Officer at Ferris State University in Big Rapids.

Don Stap has published a book of poems, *Letter at the End of Winter,* and two works of natural history prose: *A Parrot Without a Name* and *Birdsong.* A native of Michigan— where he spends part of each year—he did his undergraduate work at Western Michigan University, studying with John Woods and Herb Scott. He now teaches at the University of Central Florida.

Phillip Sterling's most recent book is *In Which Brief Stories Are Told,* a collection of short fiction. He is also the author of the poetry collection *Mutual Shores,* three chapbooks, and the editor of *Imported Breads: Literature of Cultural Exchange.* He has won an NEA Fellowship, two Fulbright Lectureships, and a PEN Syndicated Fiction Award. Retired from Ferris State University, Sterling established and coordinated the Literature In Person Reading Series.

Alison Swan is the author of two poetry chapbooks, *Before the Snow Moon* and *Dog Heart,* and the editor of *Fresh Water: Women Writing on the Great Lakes* (a Library of Michigan Notable Book). She teaches environmental thought and writing at Western Michigan University.

Keith Taylor coordinates the undergraduate creative writing program at the University of Michigan, directs the Bear River Writers' Conference, and is the poetry editor for *Michigan Quarterly Review*. He has published fourteen volumes of poetry, short fiction, translations, and edited volumes, including most recently *The Ancient Murrelet*, *If the World Becomes So Bright*, and the anthology *Ghost Writers*, co-edited with Laura Kasischke.

Matthew Thorburn is the author of three books of poems, *This Time Tomorrow*, *Every Possible Blue*, and *Subject to Change*. A native of Lansing and a graduate of the University of Michigan, he has lived and worked in New York City for more than a decade.

Russell Thorburn is the author of five books of poetry, and the forthcoming novel *Things Long Lost*. His most recent book, *Misfit Hearts*, chronicles the making of *The Misfits* through the filming-location photographs. As an artist-in-residence for the Mojave National Preserve, he created a fine art exhibit for the Desert Light Gallery, interpreting the desert in poetry.

Richard Tillinghast is the author of eleven books of poetry, most recently *Wayfaring Stranger*, and *Dirty August*, translations from the Turkish poet Edip Cansever (with Julia Clare Tillinghast). His latest non-fiction books are *Istanbul: City of Forgetting and Remembering* and *Finding Ireland*. Richard co-founded the Bear River Writers' Conference on Walloon Lake.

Rodney Torreson is the director of *Through the 3rd Eye*, an online journal that publishes the poetry of young people in the greater Grand Rapids area, and was poet laureate of Grand Rapids from 2007-2008. The author of four books, his most recent work is a chapbook entitled *The Secrets of Fieldwork*.

Robert VanderMolen lives and works in Grand Rapids, Michigan. His last collection, *Water*, was published by Michigan State University Press in 2009.

Diane Wakoski is the author of more than 20 collections of poetry. Her selected poems, *Emerald Ice*, won the William Carlos Williams prize from the Poetry Society of America. Now retired, Wakoski was Poet In Residence and University Distinguished Professor at Michigan State University 1975-2012. Her newest work, *Bay of Angels*, is forthcoming from Anhinga Press, 2013.

Daneen Wardrop is the author of a book of poetry, *The Odds of Being*, the recipient of a National Endowment for the Arts Fellowship, the Robert H. Winner Award, the Bentley Prize for Poetry, and the Gerald Cable Book Award. She has also authored three books of literary criticism, including *Emily Dickinson and the Labor of Clothing*, from University Press of New England.

Angela Knauer Williams of northern Michigan is the author of *With a Cherry on Top*, and poems, *Live From the Tiki Lounge*, from Mayapple Press. She works in the cherry industry in Leelanau County. She is an alum of Western Michigan University's theatre and writing programs, having studied with Herb Scott and John Woods.

John Woods (1926-1995) was the first faculty member to be named Distinguished Faculty Scholar at Western Michigan University, where he was a professor from 1959 until his retirement in 1992. He is the author of nine books of poetry including *The Deaths at Paragon, Indiana*; *The Valley of Minor Animals*; *The Salt Stone: Selected Poems*; and *Black Magnolias*.